RADIO'S SECOND CHANCE

RADIO'S
SECOND CHANCE

by
Charles A. Siepmann

An Atlantic Monthly Press Book

Little, Brown and Company · Boston 1947

Published April 1946
Reprinted June 1946
Reprinted April 1947

ATLANTIC–LITTLE, BROWN BOOKS
ARE PUBLISHED BY
LITTLE, BROWN AND COMPANY
IN ASSOCIATION WITH
THE ATLANTIC MONTHLY PRESS

PRINTED IN THE UNITED STATES OF AMERICA

Preface

THIS BOOK examines the performance of a great industry on which the health of our democracy depends to a degree that is frightening to the ordinary citizen who stops to think about it. It has become a bromide to say that radio is the greatest means of communication ever devised, the most potent of instruments for informing, enlightening, amusing, bemusing, confusing, or corrupting the minds and feelings of a people. The truth of it is too momentous to be allowed to fall into the limbo of accepted and unstirring platitudes.

A democracy thrives only if all its citizens are alert to the strains and dangers to which it is continuously subjected. The radio industry cannot do its job in a democratic society unless the citizens are aware of what it is doing, are alert to what it is not doing, informed enough to be intelligently critical, clearsighted enough to know responsible performance when they see it, and to demand it when they do not see it.

We must ask straight questions and look for honest answers. Who decides what we hear on the air? Who pays for it? How is what we hear affected by who pays for it? Do the people of this country get the program service they want and need, or do they not; and if not, why not? Is the electorate kept fully informed by radio about the issues on which it is being asked to make up its mind? Is there a balance of entertainment, cultural, and informational programs to feed the hungers of the majority and of the minorities whose significance a democratic state affirms? Are we getting the public service which it is our statutory right to expect? Such questions we must ask, begin to answer, and keep on asking. The wave lengths of the air belong to us, the people. Radio stations are simply the holders of temporary leases of our property. That gives us the right and the duty to keep on our toes and to watch their step.

This book is addressed to the listener, the citizen who must ask the questions and demand the answers.

Since the first and the simplest of all the misconceptions which this particular critique will be heir to is a personal one, I begin with the first person singular. For material in several chapters in this book I have drawn on studies which I made while employed, in July 1945, as special consultant to the

Federal Communications Commission. I approach all these questions with first-hand experience of both operational and policy problems in radio administration, and with special experience of broad questions concerning all the public service aspects of radio programing. But I also come to it as a former employee of the British Broadcasting Corporation. No one who is not involved in the radio business can imagine quite what a blanket of black suspicion shrouds my smallest uttèrance as a result of that fact. And because of it I am also subject to another charge which may be more generally leveled. Though an American citizen, anyone of foreign origin who undertakes criticism of an American institution is open to the obvious retort: "If you don't like it, why don't you go back where you came from?"

That is a retort that I have no intention of provoking. Criticism does not imply dislike. It is more apt to imply a troublesomely zealous concern for the institution in question. Immigrants to this country, from 1620 on, have been actively and urgently concerned with the institutions of the country of their adoption. The more recent the immigrant, the more poignant and vital his stake in the living democracy of a nation which is his not by the accident of birth but by deliberate and thoughtful choice. His hopes and expectations are perhaps sometimes greater than those of

Americans born, and correspondingly his sense of danger may be more quickly aroused than if his perspective were clouded by the comforting acceptance of familiarity. In any case, if he takes the business of his citizenship seriously, both its rights and its responsibilities, he will offer such criticisms as he may have to make in all humility, simply as one strand of his participation in the democracy's job.

The specter of a British Broadcasting past can best be exorcised by the direct approach. This book is in no sense a comparison of British and American systems of broadcasting. I do not advocate or anywhere imply that the United States would do well to adopt the British system. We certainly should not. American broadcasting stands on its merits. Our commercial system, whatever faults it may have, is the most efficient and, with due care, democratically the safest system functioning anywhere in the world. British radio has much to be said for it. But nothing that can be said for it is in any sense a menace to American radio. Very little is said about it at all in the course of this book, which is about American radio, in an American setting, with criteria of performance based on American needs and American law. It must be clearly understood that there is no underlying comparison, no lurking implication that "the British do it better." Some things the British, perhaps, do better;

many things they do very much worse. But that is another subject altogether, and neither the advantages nor the disadvantages of the British system, operating in Great Britain, are relevant here.

Nor does criticism of the abuses of the commercial system imply, by any analogy whatever, that government monopoly broadcasting is a desired alternative. Ours is a system of free enterprise within a framework of government controls, which is infinitely preferable. Radio organized by government has proved itself the most disastrous of all systems. No one who has lived in Europe could advocate that we should try that here.

The radio industry has good reason to be proud of the role that some sections of it have played, before and specially during the war. They co-operated with the government. They brought the war itself to our doors. They kept our spirits high and our attention fixed on realities. They gave us some first-class commentary as the mere mention of the names of Edward Murrow and Raymond Swing recalls. They have always given us better entertainment than radio offers in any other country in the world, and of this they are justly proud.

If this is a book of criticism of the industry's performance, it must be made perfectly clear at the beginning that there is nothing sour about it. I do not start from the premise that everything is rotten and proceed to indulge my spleen. On the contrary I start from the premise that the system is basically sound, much of the output good, some of it the best in the world. But is it good enough? Good enough for an America which is newly emerging as a world power, and whose people must know, if they are not to perish, what that means — what it means in terms of our own national life, in terms of the problems of other nations, in terms of peace or war for us or our children? We are running a race against time, in which intelligence and understanding alone can save us. Is radio helping us to win?

I do not apologize for offering criticism. A sound and healthy institution can take criticism in its stride, welcome it, and be invigorated by it. Much recent criticism of radio from listeners has been focused on "bad taste" in advertising. The _Reader's Digest_ ran an article on "radio's plug-uglies" in 1942 and got 80,000 letters from listeners disgusted with various kinds of advertising abuses. Good taste is certainly something to be desired, on the air as anywhere else. But we are not here criticizing on grounds of taste. There are other more important grounds. The state of a nation's radio is a measure of that nation's democratic health. We have seen that all too tragically illustrated in Europe and Asia where radio was, perhaps, the chief weapon used to enslave the minds and corrupt the morals of whole nations. Whether it likes to be or not, radio, in the nature of its immense power and its operation of the public's air waves, is a watchdog of democracy. It is alert, as it should be, to possibly excessive encroachments of government. Is it equally alert to dangers from within, to the dangers of abuse of freedom and default of responsibility?

A critique of radio is limited in value unless there goes with it a constructive plan. The point of this book is that there is much to be done and much that can be done. It falls, therefore, into two main parts: first, a critical analysis of what we think is wrong, and a statement of some of the things we think listeners ought to know; and second, a series of constructive proposals about what we, the listening public, and others concerned with radio, can do.

The theory we offer is quite simple. Radio is at present one-way traffic. The listener cannot answer back — effectively. He doesn't know enough about it and he isn't organized to act. If we are all of us to take our share in the molding of radio's future, we must find a way of registering our will. A two-way traffic must be organized.

But first we must get to know what is going on, and why. *We must import, as it were, the knowledge we*

*require on issues that affect us, and export, thereafter,
our considered judgments.* We shall suggest ways in
which both imports and exports can be better organized. As in everything democratic, responsibility
rests ultimately on the citizen, the voter, the con-
sumer. We can get what we like, as Bernard Shaw
puts it, or we shall grow to like what we get. It is
not too late. We can still demand what we want
from radio, if we feel that we are not being given it,
with some hope of success. The industry is sensitive
to public pressure, and certain sections of it, genuinely anxious to do a good job, would welcome a
more informed and actively interested audience.

If we are to be responsible critics of this watchdog
of democracy (responsibility must be equally distributed), we shall do well to take a broader view of
its function than the mere consideration of our likes
and dislikes of programs that we hear. We had better
consider not only the dog but what it watches. We
might take a leaf out of the book of our recent war
experiences. We fought a war so that democracy
might survive. What was so wrong with fascism that
nearly the whole world joined forces to destroy it?

For many of us fascism has come to mean personi-
fied evil. We associate it with Hitler and his rogues'
gallery and tend to overlook the fact that these war
criminals were "carriers," and only in part authors,

of the disease of fascism. What brought these crea-
tures into power? Economic, social, and political
forces were the underlying causes, but in the last
analysis it was a state of mind and a weakness of
moral fiber which permitted the Hitler and Mus-
solini gangs to take over. The German and Italian
people surrendered what we regard as inalienable
rights. They lost, in relation to the state and to society, any sense of responsible participation. Dwarfed
by the power of huge industries, the increasing, im-
personal complexity of the mechanics of government,
and the helplessness of individuals to register their
will, they drifted into political indifference and inaction.

We, too, are liable to the same kind of drift, indifference, apathy, inaction. We have not destroyed fascism. We've scotched it. It remains latent and possible, here in America as elsewhere. Its danger is
inherent in our complex modern world. We have to
keep doing something about it, or go under by default.

This brief excursion into world politics isn't as irrelevant as it may sound. Our main concern is with
the dangers to a free society which some practices in
radio exemplify. If in the context of radio we can
discover the importance of acquiring that information
and understanding which, as Lord Bacon said of

money, "is not good but it be spread," and see too the possibility of using such information for actively shaping our own future, more will have been achieved than simply the accomplishment of some "reforms" in radio. We shall have insight into our rights and our responsibilities in other fields in which our democracy remains at stake.

Democracy is not merely a form of government. It is a way of life, safeguarded, not made, by legislators. It is as important to our survival that this way of life thrive in a village as in our largest cities. If democracy should ail anywhere, its living force throughout the nation may finally become endangered.

"No man is an island, entire of itself. *Every* man is a piece of the Continent, a part of the Main. . . . *Every* man's death diminishes me, because I am involved in Mankind."

Contents

Contents

RADIO'S SECOND CHANCE

I

The Air Is Yours

WHEN RADIO programs were first offered to the public, no one had any thought of their being sponsored by advertisers. The early pioneers of radio were the manufacturers of radio equipment, electrical firms like Westinghouse and General Electric. As manufacturers, they were concerned with the making of equipment; the making of programs was a side line.

Radio programing, as we know it today, was for them simply a means of extending the sale of the receiving sets they made. It was from selling sets, not from selling time on the air, that they looked for profits. True, a very few of these firms owned patents which, in effect, also gave them a monopoly on the construction of radio transmitters. But within a few years patent rights were conceded to others and, beyond the continued ownership of certain stations, the manufacturers reverted to manufacture and new entrepreneurs undertook the making and transmission of programs.[1]

Then came the brief era of radio's gold rush, which those whose memories carry back to the middle twenties will not easily forget. The imagination of the public and of big business alike was fired by this new and extraordinary scientific miracle. Radio transmitters shot up overnight all across the country. The Department of Commerce was inundated with urgent requests for wave-length allocations. And then the Attorney General rendered an opinion that the Department was not even empowered to make such allocations. Bedlam broke loose.

Discarding all formalities, throwing prudence and restraint to the winds, new stations took to the air, stations began trespassing on one another's wave lengths, and the listener tuned in to hear competing programs superimposed on one another. And, as before and since, when unrestrained free enterprise has ended up in chaos, the public and the trade appealed to government to steer them out of it. Faced with the dissipation of their dreams of easy money and the

[1] An exception is the Radio Corporation of America, which still owns all the stock of NBC, and which appears to be pushing towards a dominant position in television broadcasting as an adjunct to its sale of television receivers. General Electric and Westinghouse are also both radio manufacturers and broadcasters.

collapse, through cutthroat competition, of their entire business, the trade sought sanctuary with the
civil servants and the ministers of state whose functions, at other times, they derided as unwarrantable
interference with the "free play of the market." "The
ether is a public medium and its use must be for
public benefit. The use of radio channels is justified
only if there is public benefit. The dominant element
for consideration in the radio field is, and always will
be, the great body of the listening public, millions in
number, countrywide in distribution." How many
listeners, one wonders, actually know of this great
inheritance?

These are the words of Mr. Herbert Hoover, to
whom, as Secretary of Commerce, it fell to unravel
the tangled skein and, with few precedents to go on,
to define the principles that should apply to the conduct of broadcasting. Later, in 1927, a temporary
agency, the Federal Radio Commission, was established to complete Mr. Hoover's work, and to complete it in six months! It is interesting to recall that,
even in the late twenties, the complex problems
raised by broadcasting were still so little realized that
a purely temporary agency was at first thought sufficient to bring us back out of bedlam.

But we learned fast and, by 1934, the Communications Act was passed, establishing a permanent regu-

latory body, the Federal Communications Commission. Of its powers and performance we shall have much to say in a later chapter. Right now, we need only note the guiding principles and wise opinions that ushered in the modern age of broadcasting and put teeth into the FCC.

The first principle, established by the Congress, was that *the people own title to the wave lengths of the air*. Private persons and commercial companies may use them as lessees for a limited period; but they have no title to them. Every owner of a radio station, before receiving a temporary license to operate, signs a waiver to any permanent claim.

The second principle follows naturally from the first: *the people's property must be protected*. And the people must be safeguarded not only from any permanent sequestration of their property, but also from intermediate abuse of it by those to whom it is temporarily ceded in trust. One hundred and thirty million people cannot take personal responsibility for the day-to-day management of their affairs, any more than can the individual shareholders of a joint stock company. It is the function of government to do this, for government alone is answerable to the people. Hence in 1934 Congress established the Federal Communications Commission as our guardian.

The terms of guardianship are clear. They define

the nature of our rights as owners of property. They define also, as we shall see, the limits of the powers of the Federal Communications Commission. Here are the terms, paraphrased from the legalistic language of the Act of Congress.[2]

The FCC is charged *to grant and, later, to renew a temporary license to operate a radio station only after it is satisfied that the applicant will operate "in the public interest, convenience or necessity."* [3] There has been much debate about the meaning of this phrase but, except to lawyers with clients to satisfy, the intention of the Congress seems perfectly clear. Times and circumstances change. Congress took account of this and used a phrase deliberately and fortunately elastic in its application. It would have been ridiculous and useless for the Congress to specify exactly and for all time what the public interest is, with respect either to the convenient allocation of wave

[2] The Communications Act reaffirmed substantially the principles defined in the Radio Act of 1927. The FCC, likewise, continued as a permanent agency the work already carried out for seven years by the temporary Federal Radio Commission which it succeeded.

[3] Note that the license is temporary, and its renewal conditioned on service to the public. Until April 1931 licenses were granted for three months only. From then until August 1939 renewal was every six months. Then, until October 1941, the maximum period for licenses was two years. Three-year licenses have only been granted since December 1943.

lengths or to the content of radio programs. Had such specification been possible, there would have been no need for a commission. The Commission is itself responsible to Congress and under annual review with regard to the renewal of its budget. It is also subject, of course, to overriding decisions in the courts. It was left, however, to build up a body of working principles, and to modify their application as time and circumstances changed.

This principle of operation "in the public interest, convenience or necessity" involved the Commission in two immediate practical tasks. The first was *to allocate wave lengths in such a manner as to provide a satisfactory program service, or choice of programs, to the largest possible number of listeners.* Local channels, regional channels, and clear channels were provided for, the first to give full and representative reflection of the local life of towns and cities, the second to cover regional interests in like manner, and the third — the clear channel stations — to reach out into rural communities remote from either local or regional stations.[4]

[4] Even so, because of physical limitations on the number of frequencies available, millions of Americans are to this day deprived of that choice of programs which they would like to have. Some have no choice at all. Even in the metropolitan districts under 300,000 only 10 out of 86 have a choice of four broadcast signals. Hardly any city half that size has

The second practical task of the Commission was *to safeguard the public against the control of stations by persons in any sense unfitted for the task of operating in the public interest.* In making application for a license it is the general practice to submit evidence of good financial standing, operating capacity, and concern for the public interest as regards the type of program service intended for the community in question.

A declaration of intentions is also normally submitted, which has this double advantage. The Commission can, in the first place, judge the merit and appropriateness of the program service proposed. A station serving a rural community is unlikely to pass muster if it disregards entirely the peculiar needs of country people. An applicant hoping to use radio for peddling some pet political or social theory, or for a quack patent medicine, will likewise not get very far. A man's professions are an earnest of his good intentions.

Secondly, the Commission has in this declaration of intentions a yardstick by which to measure the sincerity of the licensee when, after three years, his license comes up for renewal. Profession and performance can be compared, and a valid criterion is

---

four broadcasting services, and the country and small-town listener is far worse off.

established, this time on moral grounds, for judging the applicant as a servant of the public interest. If the applicant has wholly or largely failed, in actual program service, to live up to his professed intentions, unless he can show good reason why, the public is best rid of him.

And, lest it exceed the proper terms of a guardianship, Congress wisely limited the powers of the FCC itself. The Commission has no control over the selection or content of radio programs before the event, though the Communications Act expressly forbids use of obscene or profane language and publicity for lotteries on the air. No radio station need submit any script or program schedule for prior scrutiny. The Commission, indeed, is specifically debarred from censorship.

The radio industry, exploiting its vast orchestra of publicity, has again and again cried wolf at the expense of the Commission, calling it tyrant, usurper of its rights, meddlesome, interfering. In actual fact, the FCC is distinguished, so far, more for its acts of omission than those of commission. It has the meekness of the lamb, the pace and caution of the tortoise, rather than the rapacity and the swift spring of the wolf.

Today, with twenty-five years of radio experience behind us, it is interesting to ask ourselves whether, if at the start we had possessed the knowledge we now have of our own system as well as those of other countries, and if there had been a public referendum, we should have chosen differently.

We should have had to choose between four alternative systems: our own; the system of strictly government-controlled radio (as in Russia, prewar Germany, and Italy); the system adopted by Great Britain, a monopoly public service corporation; and, as in Australia and Canada, a combined system of government controlled and commercially sponsored stations. Would we have chosen any of these systems in preference to our own? The writer does not believe we would have.

Commercial radio is the natural product of our society and of our way of doing things. We believe in free competitive enterprise as the most efficient way of getting things organized and services rendered. It is the way we manufacture goods and organize our public utilities, the way we get goods and services distributed. Radio offered a new field for development to our commercial entrepreneurs and they seized on it with both hands.

The system also suits the public. Owning a set involves no tax, no irritating filling out of forms, no danger of government forcing ideas down our throats. Instead we get, or think we get, something for nothing — news programs, entertainment, and the rest. For all the discontent with advertising (part of the price we actually do pay for our commercial radio), it is questionable whether, even today, the average listener would be prepared to pay the modest price required to rid him of advertising altogether — an annual fee of approximately four dollars. For that is the estimated cost of all the programs that we hear. It includes capital outlay and depreciation costs for all the 900 and more stations on the air, their staffs, and program production costs. Jack Benny and Bob Hope, Fred Allen and Kate Smith, and all the rest of those who earn the astronomical fees paid for radio programs, could still be on the air and never a commercial from the beginning to the end, if every listener would subscribe only a little more than the cost of a cigarette a day. But the lure of an illusory something for nothing is too much for most of us. Commercial radio is in the traditional pattern of our practice and our thinking. It is the way we have organized things in the past. What was good enough for grandfather is good enough for us.

But is it? Our public officials, to their credit, early foresaw the immense, potential influence and power of radio. We have had frequent occasion to be reminded of it since. Orson Welles's program, "The Men from Mars," put half a continent in panic. The premature flash that V-E Day had come set everybody by the ears. Many have questioned whether the voicing of prejudiced opinion and biased fact, by commentators with an axe to grind, is not a serious threat to good relations and understanding among ourselves and between us and other countries.

The question, then, is this: *Is free, competitive, commercial enterprise the best and the only way to organize and to distribute information and ideas?* Are the salesmen of soap and food, drugs and tobacco, the most reliable interpreters of the kind of information and ideas on which a free, democratic people will thrive?

We have, of course, free competitive enterprise in the publication of newspapers and magazines, though freedom to publish is reserved to those few who are fortunate enough to own the vast capital required to get a paper going. But the newspaper owner does not delegate to his advertising clients power and discretion to select and sponsor the news columns, editorials, features, and comic strips that are printed. Radio networks and stations do this. It is one of the practices that we shall quarrel with.

Ideas and information are precious commodities. It would seem to follow, first, that in the public interest the advocates of our commercial system must submit to regulation beyond the self-regulation they may themselves impose; second that, in the public interest, they must be debarred from an exclusive monopoly of the field if, as is now technically possible, room can be found on the highways of the air for those whose interest in the transmission of ideas and information is other than commercial. Given these conditions, the continuance of commercial radio presents no threat to our society. We can endorse it gladly.

But the advocates of commercial radio have insisted long and loudly that there is neither need for regulation nor need for a parallel system of noncommercial broadcasting. They have paid lip service to the theory of public trusteeship, assured us that their only objective is to give the public what it wants, and claimed that they are doing so as well as, if not better than, any other agencies could do. Have they or haven't they?

The answer can only be found by examination of the facts, by comparison of profession and performance, and by a study of the philosophy behind the practice. To this end we shall examine the performance of local and clear channel stations and of our networks. Advertising and the great question of free speech will be considered, and finally we shall look at the philosophy, openly declared or clearly implied in action, of those who claim, as far as radio is concerned, that "God's in his heaven: All's right with the world."

II

Betrayal of Trust

RADIO BEGAN as a cluster of local stations, producing programs independently and drawing, almost exclusively, on local talent. In twenty years that independence has been largely forfeited and local talent has become a deserted mine. The ore, they say, has been exhausted and anyhow there are much richer seams elsewhere. And not only has the character of programs changed, but also the concept of program service. The blueprint of radio's first architects has been put aside. A trust has been betrayed in favor of a fortune.

Not only in early days (before networks, transcriptions, and wire services were heard of) but ever since, the FRC and its successor, the FCC, have placed special emphasis on local programs by local stations. Good community broadcasting has again and again been cited as one of the essential requirements of a station licensee. Assurance that "local talent will be available," that there will be "a reasonable portion of

time for programs which include religious, educational and civic matters," has influenced the Commission in its decisions to grant or renew licenses.[1] As
late as 1941 the FCC defined its policy as follows: —

> A station licensee must retain sufficient freedom of
> action to supply the program and advertising needs
> of the local community. Local program service is
> a vital part of community life. A station should be
> ready, able and willing to serve the needs of the
> local community by broadcasting such outstanding
> local events as community concerts, civic meetings,
> local sports events and other programs of local con-
> sumer and social interest.[2]

The FCC's recognition of the importance of fostering the pride and maintaining the vitality of local
communities reflects an attitude cherished throughout America and vital to the well-being of democracy.
Home-town sentiment is among the most powerful of
our emotions. But this emphasis on local life is not
derived from sentiment alone. There are sound reasons for maintaining that the future of democracy itself depends on our fostering local life as the grass
roots of our society. The American character is home-

[1] In one case the FCC's decision was reversed in the courts
when it judged the granting of a license for a station to serve
a particular community to be superfluous. The courts insisted
that the right of a community to local service be respected.

[2] *FCC Chain Broadcasting Report,* 1941.

spun. In every walk of life — in politics, in industry and commerce, in art, in sport — are to be found men and women whose talent first found outlet at the community level. As we neglect or look down on local life, so we impoverish and endanger our national vitality.

There are, moreover, dangers in the modern trend toward centralized direction and control. Whether in government or industry or in the sphere of cultural activities, this trend deprives the people of a true sense of participation. It reduces and concentrates the number of participants. Radio, unless consciously and deliberately prevented, is liable to increase this danger. It makes spectators of us all, passive recipients, through long hours, of impressions registered upon us by remote control. The local live-talent program, providing opportunity for community self-expression, can do much to forestall this trend.

Vigorous community life, again, is vital to a proper understanding of practical democracy. Democratic principles are liable to become remote and meaningless abstractions unless exemplified and practised in the circumscribed familiar field of local life. It is there that democracy's lessons are best taught. It is there that the ordinary citizen, through personal participation, may find the tangible analogies for principles and policies on which he is called to pass judgment in the wider, more complex context of national and international affairs.

It is such considerations that lend particular significance to the local service rendered by stations. Theirs is a precious trust, a unique responsibility. No consideration should override the primary objective of reflecting, fostering, developing the grass-root vitality of community spirit and of community activities. For the radio station, as we shall see, it can be profitable, too.

The local listener will, of course, want to hear and enjoy programs conceived and rendered by writers and artists more polished and sophisticated than those available in most communities — but this need not be at the expense of local life. Other criteria than purist conceptions of great art or even of slickness relate to the enjoyment and significance of programs. The local soloist, even if a little off key, may be the Tibbett of tomorrow; the village controversialist, halting in speech and unpolished in expression, may one day make history in the Congress of the United States. Peculiar interest attaches to a program just because it is local. It stands self-justified, native and personal in the emotions it evokes. Those remote from community life tend to weigh such criteria lightly.

It may, then, be instructive to examine a local community, its character, its civic interests and its social activities, and to see how effectually these are reflected in the programs of its home-town station.

Such a community is Hibbing, Minnesota, a mining town of about 16,000, retaining its original village form of government.

Hibbing's high school, built at a cost of $4,000,000, has an auditorium seating 1800, a $25,000 pipe organ, a stage 40 feet by 60 feet. The War Memorial Building covers a whole block. Its arena can be converted into a hockey rink, with space for 2400 spectators. Hibbing does things big and proud. The "village" has six municipal parks and a zoo. "A winter Sports Frolic is held in Bennett Park each February."

Its population is mixed. "Miners and lumberjacks, men from nearly every country in Europe, swarmed to the town. . . . A school was started in a store in 1893 but was housed in a building of its own the following year. Here the pupils received what was to most of them their first taste of American culture. . . . When valuable ore was found under Hibbing's streets, an iron company bought the land and in 1919 moved the village a mile farther south. Towed by log haulers, churches were slowly moved down the street — spires, pews and decorations all intact." [3] The *Hibbing Daily Tribune* now lists twenty-nine

[3] *Minnesota*, a state guide by the Federal Writers' Project of the Works Progress Administration.

churches. They have organs and choirs. They represent eleven denominations.

Hibbing has a city band, and five dance bands at
least. It has a civic music association which lately
announced a concert series with nationally known
artists. The local paper reports that "the interest and
enthusiasm already shown by a large representative
group of citizens assures success" for the series.

Hibbing has over twenty civic organizations — a
book-review club, a Teen-Age Club, a 4-H Club,
Kiwanis, Elks, Moose, Rotary.

Hibbing has professional associations, a medical
association, a building trades council, labor unions, a
chamber of commerce.

Hibbing has sports teams — softball, tennis, golf,
baseball.

Hibbing has interesting visitors. Its local paper in
June listed, among others, an eyewitness of Nazi
prison camps, a Washington correspondent, the Dean
of the University of Minnesota, the state governor, a
group of R.A.F. paratroopers, all with a story to tell.

Hibbing has problems — of municipal government,
of labor-management relations, children's and parents' problems. It has its future to worry about when
the iron ore, on which its prosperity was built, runs
out. Hibbing folk are not all of one mind. There are

differences to be reconciled, by discussion, by developing the art of human relations.

Such, and many more besides, are the components of local life. The school auditorium, the War Memorial arena, the lives, the minds, of Hibbing folk are presumably not empty. Hibbing works and plays, talks, sings and dances. What does Hibbing hear of Hibbing on the air?

The chart on page 22 lists all programs of local origin broadcast over Hibbing's one local station throughout the week beginning Sunday, January 7, 1945: —

The chart reveals the following significant facts: —

1. One fifteen-minute local live program alone occurs throughout the week after the hour of 6:00 P.M.

2. There is no local discussion period.

3. There is no program of local music.

4. All local religious broadcasts are paid for.

5. No nonprofit organization of a strictly local character is represented apart from talks on the OPA, the USES, and by the County Agent.

It may be argued that Hibbing is not a fair example by which to illustrate radio's flight from the community. Few "villages" of 16,000 population, surely, have such rich local resources. Hibbing may quite possibly be exceptional in this respect, but it is also

LIVE PROGRAMS OF LOCAL ORIGIN ON STATION WMFG

| | | No. of Minutes | |
		Commercial	Sustaining
SUNDAY			
5:30–5:45 P.M.	Radio Service Stripes ("variety")	15	
MONDAY–FRIDAY			
12:30–12:35 P.M.	News of Hibbing	25	
4:55–5:00 P.M.	News	25	
MONDAY			
5:00–5:05 P.M.	Job Reporter (USES)		5
TUESDAY			
5:00–5:15 P.M.	Gospel Tabernacle	15	
WEDNESDAY			
9:30–9:45 A.M.	Family Worship	15	
11:30–11:45 A.M.	OPA – Mrs. Reeve		15
THURSDAY			
5:00–5:05 P.M.	Job Reporter (USES)		5
FRIDAY			
9:30–9:45 A.M.	Family Worship	15	
11:35–11:45 A.M.	Itasca County Agent		10
SATURDAY			
6:30–6:45 P.M.	Gospel Tabernacle	15	
	Week's Total	125	35
	Percentage of operating time	1.7	0.6

exceptional in another. Few communities of its size have a local station all to themselves. The large majority of stations cover much wider areas and much bigger populations. The average amount of talent and the range of local interests to be developed are, therefore, much greater than in Hibbing.

Or again it may be objected that Hibbing represents an extreme example of default by a local station. The default is indeed extreme, but not many
stations fare very much better. The present pauper
status of local programs on all classes of stations is
illustrated in the following chart: —

AVERAGE HOURS PER DAY DEVOTED TO LOCAL, LIVE
PROGRAMS BY CLASS OF STATION

For Month of January, 1945

	Commercial Hours Per Day	Sustaining Hours Per Day
50-kw. stations (41)	3:02	1:52
500-w–50-kw. stations (214)	2:23	1:11
250-w or less stations (376)	1:43	1:00
Part-time stations (72)	2:11	1:09
All stations (703)	2:02	1:07
6 P.M. TO 11 P.M. ONLY		
50-kw. stations (41)	:36	:12
500-w–50-kw. stations (214)	:34	:14
250-w or less stations (376)	:29	:15
Part-time stations (72)	:11	:07
All stations (703)	:29	:13

Thus — *a.* In no class of station is as much as an average
of two hours a day reserved for local sustaining programs.

b. In all classes of station, with one exception, the
total average time reserved in the entire day
for local sustaining programs barely exceeds
one hour.

    c. Between the hours of 6 and 11 P.M., the *maximum* average time, in any class of station, reserved for local sustaining programs is 15 minutes.

    d. Between the hours of 6 and 11 P.M., in *all* classes of stations, the total average time for local programs, commercial *or* sustaining, is 42 minutes.

The presence or absence of local talent, however, and the size of the community served by a station, are irrelevant considerations if we are looking for the cause of this development of ghost towns on the air. There are other reasons. Local stations have found easier means of making money and, with some honorable exceptions, they have followed the line of least resistance. This has taken two forms — excessive reliance on network programs, and excessive use of transcriptions and recorded programs. Turning their backs on service to their communities, they have gone after easy money and made plenty of it.

Networks programs, as we shall acknowledge handsomely in the next chapter, have enormously enriched our radio services. They are here to stay and we should be the poorer without them. A good case can even be made for their monopoly of a large part of the time on the air of stations affiliated with them — but this, surely, must be short of the virtual exclusion of local live programs (programs originating in the locality and using live talent).

Hibbing provides an interesting example of the virtual monopoly of good evening listening time by programs fed to the local station by a network. Thus, on Sunday night of the week alluded to above, between 6 and 11 P.M. all but fifteen minutes were devoted to programs originated by NBC. But again, lest Hibbing be thought exceptional, let us examine the statistics for all stations of all sizes.

Let us note, first, the number of stations affiliated with networks and contractually bound by them to take stated amounts of network originated programs. Of approximately 940 stations in America over 600 are affiliated with one or other of the four great networks. In the main evening hours network affiliated stations use nearly 95 per cent of broadcasting power.[4]

In these main evening hours to what extent are the affiliated stations mere "feeders" for programs origi-

---

[4] During daytime hours a much bigger percentage of stations is in the "nonaffiliated" category. This is because many small local stations are on "limited time" — that is, have to go off the air at sundown so as to preclude interference, which is greater after dark, with other stations. Stations on limited time are not a profitable investment for networks which have their eyes on the mass evening audiences, and are therefore, most of them, nonaffiliated "local" stations in the strict and original sense of the term.

nated outside the local community by the parent network? The following facts give a graphic picture of how things stand as illustrated by a typical Sunday in April, 1944: —

On NBC, 28 "basic"[5] affiliated stations provide, between them, only one period of 15 minutes for non-network programs between 7 and 11 P.M.

On Mutual, 23 out of 33 stations provide only 15 minutes for non-network programs between 6 and 11 P.M.

On CBS, 12 of the basic stations have no time at all for any non-network program between 6 and 11 P.M.; one station concedes five minutes.

On the Blue Network 16 of the basic stations have only 15 minutes of non-network programs between 6 and 11 P.M.

On our two largest and oldest networks approximately 85 per cent (on NBC) and 89 per cent (on CBS) of the main evening hours were devoted to national *commercial* programs, and approximately 9 per cent and 8 per cent, respectively, to non-network programs, whether commercial or sustaining.

Nor have we any guarantee that of this meager remnant time (or of the greater amount of remnant time on the Blue and Mutual Networks) all was devoted to truly local programs. For "local" programs

[5] Basic affiliated stations constitute a nucleus of stations on a network on which any advertiser has to buy time, regardless of how many other "supplementary" stations he may choose to buy.

include phonograph records, transcriptions,[6] and the reading of syndicated wire news services which are local only in the sense that an announcer at the local station reads them, or in so far as they include an item or two of local news.

Thus of the meager time allotted to locally originated programs an undetermined but considerable proportion is local only in a quite fictitious sense. It originates in, but in no way bespeaks or reflects, the local community.

Why do we have this imbalance between local and nonlocal programs? There is no simple answer to the question. Local stations rightly feel that their listeners will want to hear the best network programs. Then contracts with the networks bind them in any case to a variable extent to take the sponsored network programs. Or look at it from a network's point of view. A network, if it is to attract national advertisers, must be able to guarantee a sufficient "coverage" (must, in other words, be able to assure a sponsor that a stated number of affiliated stations will carry the program) to make it worth while to the sponsor to invest his money.

All this is granted. But when networks so dominate

---

[6] A transcription is a recording made specially for broadcasting use, as distinct from a record prepared for sale to the public.

the local scene, or when affiliated stations so choose to pre-empt their time in favor of their parent network as to reduce local programs to marginal proportions, we have reached a pretty pass. Local stations survive, under these conditions, in name only, and the philosophy we have advanced and the reiterated policy of the FCC to uphold the rights and interests of local communities go by default. Local affiliated stations secure a comfortable income from their share of the national advertiser's payment for time, but their role is reduced to that of sleeping partners in a concern whose enterprise and initiative originate elsewhere. Local stations were not given licenses to act as tollkeepers on a bridge that others built.

The blame for our present situation is probably divided. Networks have been overeager to incorporate more and more stations for longer and longer hours as mere relay points for their sponsored programs. Local affiliates have fallen too easily for the bait of easy money, have conceded too much of independence, and have, moreover, defaulted even in the remnant time still free for a display of local initiative.

We shall have occasion, in a later chapter, to speak up for the transcribed and recorded program. Here we are concerned with its misuse, which takes the form of an excessive use at the expense of other programs.

On nonaffiliated stations the prevalent excess of recorded programs is particularly marked, and the reason is not far to seek. They cost little, they are convenient vehicles for profitable "spot" announcements, and they tax no one's ingenuity. Using records and transcriptions only, a local station can, virtually, be run by an announcer and an engineer. There is one actual instance of a station that, to all intents and purposes, adopted this easy-money formula. While an extreme example, it illustrates a general practice against which there has been far too little protest.

On May 22, 1939, Station KIEV in Glendale, California, filed application for renewal of its license. The station had been given a construction permit seven years previously when it pleaded its desire to serve the local community (and incidentally asked that, to make room for it, an existing station in the area should have its facilities withdrawn).

Back in 1932 the station management was very clear about its devotion to the public interest. It proposed to operate the station as a civic project, claimed that the Chamber of Commerce and several civic organizations had said an urgent need existed for such a station, promised to co-operate with local organizations by donating them time, said that one third of the broadcasting time would be reserved for educational and semieducational subjects, that 20 per cent of its time would be for sustaining programs and that Glendale had "excellent talent" available. But seven years is a long time; memory fades and old promises grow dusty. When FCC monitors checked the programs put out in 1939, this is what they found.

On the first of three days during which programs were recorded by the FCC, "the programs consisted of 143 popular records and nine semi-classical records. There were 264 commercial announcements and three minutes of announcements concerning lost and found pets."

On the second day the programs consisted of "156 popular and 10 semi-classical records and were accompanied by 258 commercial announcements. Ten minutes were devoted to the lost and found pet column."

On the third day the same general picture obtained. *"During these three days, which represented a total of 36 hours of broadcast time, only 23 minutes were devoted to programs other than records and commercial announcements."*

For a period of over a year it was found that no regular news was broadcast over the station. *"Each five-minute program contains at least one commercial announcement and some recorded music."*

For reasons best known to themselves the FCC approved renewal of the station's license in 1940 on a showing of a desire to do better next time. But four years later, in 1944, the station's programs for the week of April 23 showed that more than 88 per cent of its time was still being used for mechanically reproduced music. Less than 3.7 per cent of its time (or 30 minutes a day) was being used to display the "excellent talent" available to consummate this civic project. The local live-talent programs consisted of one singer who sang for 15 minutes six times a week, one pianist for 15 minutes on Saturday, one 15-minute school program, and a devotional program daily, except Sunday.

Station KIEV is somewhat of an exception to the rule, but the rule itself is disturbing. In January 1945, in over 763 stations of all types, approximately five hours a day were being devoted to recorded and transcribed programs. In two important station categories, comprising 590 stations, approximately one fifth or more of the five peak evening hours from 6 to 11 P.M. were recorded.

During the daytime the situation is worse. Not only are hours of precious time devoted to recordings which might be given to useful and popular local service programs, but on many stations a vicious kind of exploitation is now prevalent. We allude to the "Captain Cash" type of program in which records are spun for consecutive hours a day, not with a view to entertainment but to bribing listeners to keep their ears pricked for the "commercials" with which these programs abound. Listeners are awarded cash simply for having their sets tuned in when called up on the telephone. In these programs the content and interest of what is broadcast are deliberately subordinated to the purpose of inducing listeners, by a monetary appeal, to subject themselves over long periods of time to sales appeals. The FCC has not yet thought fit to comment on the public interest, convenience, and necessity here served.

On nonaffiliated stations a moderate use of recorded programs need not (and in some cases does not) conflict with adequate reflection of community life. On affiliated stations, committed by contract to carry varying amounts of network commercial programs, the use of recorded programs merely adds to their burden and further narrows the margin of time available for live local programs. Here it is the *combined* effect of the use of network and recorded programs that we must watch if we are to judge the present extent of service, actual or potential, to the local community. The following charts show where we stand: —

RATIO OF HOURS FOR NETWORK AND RECORDED PROGRAMS
TO PROGRAMS OF LOCAL ORIGIN IN WEEK OF
JANUARY 2, 1945

A. ALL HOURS

	All Stations	50-kw. Stations	5–50 kw. Stations	250 w. or Less Stations	Part-time Stations
Network	7:43	10:25	8:59	7:52	2:21
Recorded	5:13	3:45	4:54	5:40	5:08
Total network and recorded	12:56	14:10	13:53	13:32	7:29
Local (including syndicated wire news)	3:10	4:54	3:33	2:47	3:20

B. 6–11 P.M.

	All Stations	50-kw. Stations	5–50 kw. Stations	250 w. or Less Stations	Part-time Stations
Network	2:47	3:43	3:14	2:49	3:29
Recorded	1:06	:29	:58	1:21	:30
Total network and recorded	3:53	4:12	4:12	4:10	:59
Total local	:43	:48	:48	:44	:18

Look at the figures for evening hours after 6 P.M., the only time of day when men and women alike are apt to be at home and in a mood to listen. Is it enough that forty-five minutes of an evening should be reserved for locally originated programs including wire news programs? The reader alone can judge, from his own knowledge of the needs of his community and from his own experience of local programs offered over his local station.

Local programs do not just happen. They are conceived, planned, written, and produced. All this involves talent and time. In many communities talent is there, awaiting only the encouragement and guidance of a radio professional. At how many local stations is such expert supervisory assistance available? How many local stations have talent scouts, producers, writers, capable either of originating or at least of helping to originate such programs as Hibbing had to offer?

In April 1944 834 stations employed 863 writers at an average salary of $40.14 a week. Significantly these same stations employed 1195 commercial salesmen, at an average salary of $95.92 a week.

There were 415 local stations which employed 259 writers full time, at an average salary of $31.87, but employed 409 salesmen at an average salary of $68.85 a week.

The average local station employed less than one third of a full-time musician and less than one sixth of a full-time actor. One wonders what these dismembered human entities produced.

Such figures speak for themselves. It is easier and more profitable to spin platters and block out a program chart with the bulk of evening hours marked "reserved for network programs." It is easier and more profitable to send out salesmen to pull in spot announcements to be interspersed in intervals between records. It all adds up to a lot of easy money and to very little sense — from the public's point of view.

The alternative is not altruism and self-denial and bankruptcy. On the contrary, there is good reason to believe that local programs are good business, as well as good public service. Given imagination, it may mean the reverse of bankruptcy — the discovery of a gold mine, as the following story illustrates.

One 250-watt station located in the Middle West had struggled along for four years and lost money each year until a reorganization was forced in 1942. "The former management had attempted to compete directly with outside stations whose signals were strong in the local community. Good entertainment was provided but no attempt was made to establish the station as a local institution interested in the life of the community. Neither local listeners nor local businessmen supported the station.

"The new management reversed this policy completely. All attempts at competing with outside stations were eliminated. The management not only studied the activities peculiar to that community, but also took a personal interest in them. Station facilities were made available on a free basis to civic institutions such as the Chamber of Commerce,

Women's Clubs, Parent-Teachers Association, public schools and Community Chest. School sport contests were broadcast, and other programs of distinctly local interest were developed. In a relatively
short time, an audience of more than 50 per cent of
all local radio listeners had been attracted to the station. . . . At the time the new management came
in, gross monthly income was $2,400. At the end of
12 months the amount had been increased to $6,000.
The new manager attributed all improvement to the
policy of making the station a real local institution
and a true voice of the community." [7]

The imagination shown by this station was not
extreme. It leaves each of us plenty of room for
thinking of other programs that might have matched
and indeed outmatched those provided. The mine
of talent is not exhausted. In many localities it has
not yet been opened up. There is no one to dig. The
salesmen are on the road looking for "spots." The
one fifth of a musician is playing on a fiddle with one
string.

Local talent, unaided and inexperienced, occasionally limps up to a microphone and brings discredit
on local programs by a lame, amateur performance. [8]

[7] C. H. Sandage, *Radio Advertising for Retailers,* Harvard
University Press, 1945, p. 210.

[8] This, however, is far from being the rule. A number of
nonprofit organizations are nowadays producing their own

Its lack of polish is then made the basis of a claim that amateurs cannot compete in the brisk, competitive field of modern professional radio. Unaided, they normally cannot. But the blame is being placed in the wrong place. It should be laid squarely at the door of local stations that fail their communities by falling down on their own job. A positive responsibility rests upon local stations to make articulate the voice of the community. Unless time is earmarked for such a purpose, unless talent is actively sought and given at least some degree of expert assistance, the flower of local vitality is likely to wither on the stem or be transplanted to Hollywood or some other center that provides the lure of sunshine and opportunity.

Some stations (unfortunately they are a minority) have seen that profits and public service at the community level are not incompatible. Station KSTP, St. Paul, Minnesota, put on the commencement program of a local high school. Its success was so great that it was later repeated and carried over the NBC Network. "America Calling" is now recorded and a permanent addition to our national cultural resources.

---

programs. In 1945 they carried off a high proportion of the first awards made by the Ohio Institute on Radio in Education.

Or take another example. Amateur shows have been used effectively in developing local talent. "An Illinois retailer has used this type of show for years and has built an audience which in 1942 surpassed the audience for any other program broadcast at the same time. . . . It was competing with John Charles Thomas, the New York Philharmonic and the Army Hour. Only the first of these even approached the rating of the local program." [9]

One may question whether this program achieved the "cultural" heights or the professional slickness of those competing programs. But radio, which claims it gives the people what it wants, has failed to reckon with that facet of human interest and loyalty to which we alluded earlier. Good local programs stand self-justified and assured of a response just because they are local.

The popularity of certain local stations over competing networks would seem to prove that point. A study of the comparative daytime popularity of different kinds of stations was made by NBC. In general, as was to be expected, most families approached in the survey named a station affiliated with a network. Seeing that substantially all of the more powerful stations are affiliated with a network,

[9] Sandage, *op. cit.*, pp. 166–167.

it could hardly be otherwise. But the survey makes it clear that, particularly in cities where there is an unaffiliated station providing good local programs, unaffiliated stations may eclipse the popularity of network stations.

Thus in Dothan, Alabama, 79 per cent said that they "listened most" during the day to a non-network station. In Tuscaloosa 59 per cent gave a like response. In 43 other towns and cities stations not affiliated with any network outranked stations affiliated with one or other of the four networks. Home-town sentiment and interest apparently survives here and there despite the centralizing influence of radio. But if it depended for sustenance on radio alone, its life prospects would be short indeed.

Approximately a quarter of our population lives on farms. Nearly another quarter lives in small country towns. Radio's first architects planned that these listeners should be served. Realizing that local commercial stations would tend to concentrate in thickly populated areas (where profits on advertising would be highest), they provided for powerful clear channel stations to reach out into country districts and serve them according to their needs.

The plan misfired. It was not possible to blanket rural areas with sure signals to the same extent as has proved possible in big urban centers. More than one third the area of the United States, with a population of 10 million, or only a little less than the total population of Canada, is without any daytime radio service at all. More than half the area of the United States, with a population of some 21 million, has to rely on relatively inferior "secondary" or "skywave" service at night. The clear channel stations have in any case failed to provide for country listeners' special needs and interests. They have offered urban fare, much of it, of course, entirely palatable, but the rural market, as such, remains to this day underfed.

It is hardly surprising, then, that rural listeners, as compared with town listeners, are few and that much dissatisfaction exists. According to the 1940 census, only 60.2 per cent of all farm dwellings were equipped with radios, as compared with 91.9 per cent of urban dwellings. Poverty no doubt is among the factors contributing to this striking contrast in market saturation, but poor reception and poor program service are others.

The country listener is particularly hard hit by the trend we have examined toward network affiliation and the use of transcribed and recorded programs. His needs are the first to be discounted. Local farm broadcasts yield to the more profitable network programs sponsored by national advertisers. Here is an example, one of many, of what happens: —

The Texas Livestock Marketing Association for seven years sponsored an afternoon livestock broadcast at 3:25 P.M. over Station KTSA, San Antonio, Texas. This program served a real need and was widely listened to by ranchers who needed to know the market at that time so they could round up cattle to drive to market early the next day. Early in February of this year, KTSA informed the Livestock Marketing Association that their time had been sold to another commercial program. Vigorous protest by the co-operative to the station brought no results, but when 62 irate letters were filed with the FCC . . . KTSA did an about face and restored the program. It is conceivable that KTSA was aware of the fact that hearings on rural radio service begin in September.[10]

In a survey recently undertaken the following opinions were expressed. Of those replying, 57 per cent believed that clear channel stations did not carry satisfactory farm programs; 48 per cent believed that commercial programs were crowding farm programs into less desirable listening times.

The farmer, like other listeners, is getting great

[10] Statement by C. Maurice Wieting at the New York State Institute of Community Service, July 6, 1945.

benefits from radio today. No one doubts it. But the question is whether he is getting that modest provision for his special interests and needs to which he should be entitled. Here, as in all that we have said, our concern is with full and sufficient service to communities compatible with reasonable profits for the broadcaster. All the evidence seems to suggest that profits far outrun the benefits and services conferred by those who make them. Thirty minutes a day on each clear channel station devoted to the distinctive needs of our farm population, during hours when it can hear, hardly seems an exorbitant demand. Yet that is what most clear channel stations are still failing to provide.

We believe, then, that local stations, by virtually selling their birthright to the networks or by seeking a short cut to profits by the misuse and excessive use of records, are in fact cutting off their nose to spite their face. Their safest investment in the long run is in their local market. Networks are, as we shall see, far too heavily committed to a small and powerful group of advertisers to offer their affiliates gilt-edged security. The boom days cannot last. The local station cannot forever thrive apart from the community it serves, just as the community cannot realize its full potentialities without the active help and interest of its local station.

A station which sells its community down the river will find at last that it has also sold out on its own advertisers. Radio can only thrive as it makes talent thrive, and the more widespread and dispersed the flowering of new talent, the more broadly the risks of radio are spread. We suggest that local stations reverse their present policies, look to their local markets, call in their salesmen, send out their talent scouts, make each of their stations a market and a milieu for live talent (in terms of script writers and producers capable of transforming the local scene into programs of interest and artistic merit) instead of a mere booster point for programs from afar or a booth for spinning platters.

We admit the problem of reconciling local needs and interests with wider interests and needs for which network programs have, at their best, created a well-merited demand. But the problem is not insuperable. There is, yet, as we have tried to show, a lot of slack to take up. The reservation of even 15 per cent of time, in each of the three main segments of the day, for locally originated programs would neither interfere with listeners' demands for network service nor cripple profits. On the contrary, profits might well increase. The public is already restive at the abuse of advertising. It would respond with enthusiasm to advertisers offering a reasonable *quid pro quo* for their present pitiless assault on our ears and sensibilities.

The restiveness, of which we shall cite examples throughout this book, will spread unless abuse is checked. The measure of necessary government control is the default of private industry.

III

The Networks Abdicate

Broadcasting stations are licensed to serve the
public and not for the purpose of furthering the private or selfish interests of individuals or groups of
individuals. The standard of public interest, convenience, or necessity means nothing if it does not
mean this. . . . The emphasis should be on the *receiving* of service and the standard of public interest, convenience, or necessity should be construed
accordingly. . . . The *entire* listening public within
the service area of a station, or of a group of stations in one community, is entitled to service. In a
sense a broadcasting station may be regarded as a
sort of mouthpiece on the air for the community it
serves, over which its public events of general interest, its political campaigns, its election results,
its athletic contests, its orchestras and artists, and
discussion of its public issues may be broadcast. *If
. . . the station performs its duty in furnishing a well
rounded program, the rights of the community have
been achieved.*[1]

[1] *In re* Great Lakes Broadcasting Co.: Federal Radio Commission, Docket No. 4900; 3rd Annual Report, 1928.

THUS THE Federal Radio Commission in 1928, when network broadcasting was still a new, untried adventure. The National Broadcasting Company was formed in 1927, the Columbia Broadcasting System a year later. A generation has grown up since for which radio means, primarily, network service. Nor are those with longer memories likely to be shedding tears now for the good old days.

ᐧ In less than twenty years the networks have raised the standards, extended the subject range and the number of the programs that we hear, at a speed and with an alert efficiency that are breathtaking. The public's favorite programs are, with rare exceptions, network programs; the best commentators are network men; a world war broke out and network correspondents were at once on every front. Long before our own entry into the war, network reporters were bringing its import home to us in responsible and often moving terms. The networks have given us not only nationwide but world-wide coverage. The stamp of network enterprise is indelibly imprinted on our system of broadcasting and, with all its defects, it is the best system and the best service in the world.

But this is America, where men are accustomed to speak their minds and where society and all its institutions thrive on a healthy discontent. We may have the best broadcasting on earth, but is it good enough — for America? With sincere and generous acknowledgment of an amazing record of achievement, and with a full awareness of the bewildering complexity of organizing radio for a subcontinent, let us consider some remediable defects and acquaint ourselves with certain trends which, unless scotched, may deprive us of the lead in what are still the pioneer days of broadcasting.

"The emphasis should be on the *receiving* of service . . . the *entire* listening public . . . is entitled to service." To what extent does this obtain? In the last chapter we traced the decline of service to communities by local stations. Among the reasons noted was their surrender to networks of their birthright of local initiative. How far have networks made good this loss by themselves giving us programs sufficiently diverse to satisfy other needs and interests?

Network broadcasting was a brilliant idea. By associating local stations all over the country with a central programing agency, it seemed feasible to combine the advantages of local broadcasting with those of a national service of programs. There should be room for both.

But how could a network finance the ambitious program service that was contemplated? Two necessary steps had to be taken. Advertisers had to be persuaded that national advertising by radio would pay, and, once persuaded, they had to be guaranteed approximate nationwide coverage for the program they undertook to sponsor. That is, the network had to secure a web of local stations, contractually engaged to take the advertiser's programs. The two steps were taken in parallel. Over the years radio advertising was shown progressively to be a paying proposition, and more and more stations were persuaded to affiliate themselves with networks on the terms necessary to attract the custom of the advertiser.

By the end of 1943 more than two thirds of the commercial stations had become affiliates of one or other of the four major networks, and the lining up of local stations was still going on apace. During the year the Blue Network added 33 affiliates and Mutual 15. Now, more than 600 stations which together use nearly 95 per cent of nighttime broadcasting power are network affiliates.

Network affiliation is a very profitable undertaking. The local affiliate gets a percentage of the national advertiser's fee simply by reserving time on his station for the program. He gets money virtually for nothing. No wonder, then, that so many stations have in effect gone out of business as local station operators and become mere feeding stations for the networks. A progressive domination over their affiliated stations by the parent networks developed which, by 1939, had become so great that the FCC, at the insistence of Congress, began an investigation and thereafter issued Chain Broadcasting Regulations intended to curb what it was feared might be monopoly control in radio.[2]

Networks were not only attracting local stations into their orbit of control but they were buying stations for themselves. True, the largest number owned by any network is nine, but one whale of a station is worth a lot of minnows. There is a world of difference between a 250-watt station whose signal barely reaches the horizon and a 50,000-watt clear channel station which sends its signal nightly into over half the states in the Union. Of such clear channel stations there are 46. One third of these are owned by NBC and CBS. *The stations thus owned occupy twice as much space in the radio spectrum as all our 444 local stations combined.*

The networks are thus very powerful groups. They are also very rich. They have a right to be, for they

---

[2] At the time, networks protested that the FCC's regulations meant their ruin and the end of our system of broadcasting. In actual practice the situation has been virtually unaffected. NBC was forced to sell the Blue Network but, for the rest, broadcasting and the relations between networks and affiliates have continued pretty much as before.

have been the pacemakers of radio's financial progress. How hot the pace has been few listeners probably realize.

Radio has been a boom town for a long time now. Beginning modestly in 1927, the gross figure for the sale of time on the air was less than $5,000,000. Five years later, in 1932, it was about thirteen times higher, or $62,000,000. Another five years later, it had doubled, amounting to $144,000,000; and in yet another five years, by 1943, it had yet again more than doubled, amounting to an all-time high of $307,-000,000. The next year, 1944, was better still, and 1945 may beat all previous records. *Gross receipts thus increased more than sixty times in less than twenty years.*

The lion's share of the profits from these gross receipts has gone to the great networks. How much of them has been turned back into programs, to provide the program diversity due to "the entire listening public"?

Figures provide the least satisfactory answer to the question. Simpler and more convincing is a glance at the radio log in your morning newspaper, or a turn of your dial at any time of the day or night. There are four great networks to choose from, all of them competing feverishly with one another. Check their performance at any given time. Is it diversity of choice that is being offered?

To judge fairly, we need some definition of desirable diversity. The reader is invited to make his own, but here is one, applicable to networks, which we might use as a rough test of what we might expect to receive.

WHAT IS GOOD PROGRAM SERVICE?

Since all listeners cannot tune in at all times of the day, we might expect that in each of the three main segments of the day — morning, afternoon, and evening — we should have programs of the following types: —

1. News, national and international, with informed and responsible interpretation and comment.

2. Varied entertainment, including light and serious drama.

3. Programs on national and international issues, affecting the well-being of democracy, fairly discussed or effectively dramatized or simply explained. Democracy at work, both in the past (to keep us alive to our heritage) and in the present; the great issues before Congress; social issues affecting us all — problems of health, of education, and of social better-

ment, such as the cure of unemployment, and good housing.

4. Programs of interest to large and important sections of the community everywhere — women's interests (particularly during daytime hours, when they constitute the majority of listeners); farmers' interests; the interests of employers and of labor; children's interests — the best that can be given; religious interests, and so on.

5. Programs for significant "cultural" minorities, not to be discounted just because they are few, but fostered and catered for because they may be the majority of an enlightened tomorrow; lovers of music and of literature, listeners curious about science and its discoveries.

We need not look for an *equal* amount of programs in each category. We *should* look for a continuous flow from each of these abundant springs, the flow perhaps regulated more or less in a descending order corresponding to our list. The days are long, and they follow one another. The time available is not an obstacle to rich diversity. How many of these categories are regularly covered in network programs? Again the reader is asked to judge. But an example may help to show not only how, but why, the theory that making good is tantamount to doing good breaks down.

*   *   *

Had you turned, in the spring of 1945, to the schedules of our two oldest and richest networks you would have found, among others, the following programs listed: —

NBC *

Monday–Friday	Program	Percentage of Available Audience Listening
10:15–10:30 A.M.	"Lora Lawton"	4.4
10:30–10:45 A.M.	"Road of Life"	4.0
10:45–11:00 A.M.	"Joyce Jordan"	4.1
11:45–12:00 M.	"David Harum"	4.0
2:00–2:15 P.M.	"Guiding Light"	8.1
2:15–2:30 P.M.	"Today's Children"	8.9
2:30–2:45 P.M.	"Women in White"	8.5
3:00–3:15 P.M.	"A Woman of America"	7.0
3:15–3:30 P.M.	"Oxydol's Own Ma Perkins" . .	9.2
3:30–3:45 P.M.	"Pepper Young's Family"	10.7
3:45–4:00 P.M.	"Right to Happiness"	10.5
4:00–4:15 P.M.	"Backstage Wife"	9.9
4:15–4:30 P.M.	"Stella Dallas"	10.2
4:30–4:45 P.M.	"Lorenzo Jones"	9.8
4:45–5:00 P.M.	"Young Widder Brown"	10.7
5:00–5:15 P.M.	"When a Girl Marries"	12.5
5:15–5:30 P.M.	"Portia Faces Life"	11.0
5:30–5:45 P.M.	"Just Plain Bill"	8.9
5:45–6:00 P.M.	"Front Page Farrell"	7.5

CBS †

10:00–10:15 A.M.	"Valiant Lady"	3.8
10:15–10:30 A.M.	"Light of the World"	4.9
10:30–10:45 A.M.	"The Strange Romance of Evelyn Winters"	4.5

* Source: NBC Advance Program Schedule, week of April 29, 1945.

† Source: CBS Program Book, May 1, 1945.

CBS (*Continued*)

Monday–Friday	Program	Percentage of Available Audience Listening
10:45–11:00 A.M.	"Bachelor's Children"	5.8
11:00–11:15 A.M.	"Amanda"	3.8
11:15–11:30 A.M.	"Second Husband"	4.5
11:30–11:45 A.M.	"Bright Horizon"	6.2
12:15–12:30 P.M.	"Big Sister"	9.3
12:30–12:45 P.M.	"The Romance of Helen Trent"	9.7
12:45–1:00 P.M.	"Our Gal Sunday"	9.6
1:00–1:15 P.M.	"Life Can Be Beautiful"	10.2
1:15–1:30 P.M.	"Ma Perkins"	11.0
1:45–2:00 P.M.	"Young Dr. Malone"	7.5
2:00–2:15 P.M.	"Two on a Clue"	6.3
2:15–2:30 P.M.	"Rosemary"	6.1
2:30–2:45 P.M.	"Perry Mason"	5.8
2:45–3:00 P.M.	"Tena & Tim"	5.7

What are these programs? They are all "soap operas," or serial dramatic programs in which, by design, "an understanding of today's episode is dependent upon previous listening." They appear in the programs five days a week. They continue from week to week. At least one has been turning out new, daily "episodes" for ten consecutive years. They vary in subject and treatment but many conform broadly to the standards set by one of the oldest and most successful soap-opera librettists, Miss Irna Phillips. Of her work a writer has said: "The writing, direction and playing are in the most intense terms. The tone is lugubrious and the pace is torpid. There is never the slightest suggestion of lightness or enjoyment, but the emphasis is constantly on emotional contortion, and mental anguish."

Here are some of her soap operas described in miniature: —

> In "Lonely Women," a girl, secretly married to a man accused of being a Nazi spy, has gone away to have her baby. There is also a strong hint of an illegitimate child in the past of a mother who doesn't know the daughter she is visiting. In "Women in White" there was an illegitimate baby, whose mother fooled her newly married husband into thinking it was his. And about the time the serial went off the air, this child was mutilated in an accident. In "Right to Happiness" a girl married the man her mother loved, then divorced him. When he told her second husband of her past, she killed him, went to prison for murder and gave birth to a baby there.

"Over the last few years, Miss Phillips' stories have contained a variety of brutal physical situations, divorces, illegitimate births, suggestions of incest and even murders." [3]

Not all soap operas by any means are of this kind but in general their tone remains "lugubrious and the pace torpid." Listeners who refuse to tune in to them give, as their chief reason, that they want to be cheered and not depressed, soothed and not

[3] Hobe Morrison in *Variety*, August 18, 1943.

whipped up daily to a tense pitch of excitement and anxiety.

The number of soap operas is less today than it used to be, but as our list suggests, it is still fairly generous. On NBC they occupy all but three and one-quarter hours between ten in the morning and six at night; on CBS all but three and three-quarters hours.

Who listens to them? According to a survey of these programs, as broadcast between December 1944 and April 1945, less than 10 per cent of the audience available at home tuned in to any one of these programs at any given time. (See individual percentages in the last column of the chart on page 54.) The remaining listeners either listened to other programs or had their sets switched off altogether.

Many people have strong opinions about the merits of soap operas. Why people listen to them and what cravings they satisfy have been studied by competent research workers, and some of their conclusions are not reassuring with regard to the sturdiness of democratic morale. But rather than obtrude a personal judgment, let us ask ourselves a more relevant question. The industry justifies itself by claiming that it gives the public what it wants. Why then do our two greatest networks continue to fill daytime listening hours with programs which investigation proves to be unpopular with, or disregarded by, the majority of available listeners? We cannot be sure of the answer, but some indisputable facts suggest a clue.

In the first place, soap operas are relatively cheap programs to produce. Their authors are not the highest paid, their casts are small, and the actors and actresses are not stars as are those who sell the great audience-gathering programs heard in the evening. The advertiser, therefore, is put to relatively small expense to get his commercial message across.

Soap operas, secondly, are especially convenient vehicles for advertising plugs. No other type of program heard is so heavily loaded, fore and aft and in between, with advertising copy. A typical fifteen-minute program contains only eight or nine or so minutes of soap opera. Six or seven minutes intervene between the end of one and the beginning of the next. The great majority of this intervening time consists of advertising plugs.

Again, the suspense and excitement of the serial, as it is unfolded, create a peculiar attentiveness. Listeners are addicts of an almost morbid character. Their attention, therefore, is easily transferred to the plug, giving it a peculiarly powerful selling property.

Sometimes one of the actors steps out of character

to bespeak the commercial message. The persuasiveness of this appeal can readily be understood when we recall that these fictional characters are very far from fictitious — to this morbid coterie of listeners. Soap operas, for many of them, are more real than life itself. Many of these listeners *escape* from life into the world of fantasy and daydreams that many soap operas deliberately offer. The characters are not voices at a microphone, but the men and women the listener wishes she herself was or, alternatively, the living projection of the listener's own thwarted dreams, frustrations, and personal anxieties. Is it to be wondered, then, that when this personification of the listener's deepest frustration for a moment bespeaks a product, in the same soothing and intimate tones used in the enactment of the drama, the appeal comes with the authority, almost, of Almighty God?

Here, perhaps, is a third clue to the continuing monopoly of so many daytime hours by the soap operas, loathed or neglected by the majority of listeners. The intense interest of the addicts, their morbid frame of mind, their pitiable credulity, make them a pushover for the advertiser. And given the program policy defined for us by one great network president — "We are selling time for one specific reason, and that is to sell goods" — no type of program better fulfills its purpose.

Soap operas sell goods. That is why they continue. For the advertiser, naturally, is interested not in the *total* size of his audience but in that section of it on which he can prevail to make a purchase. An audience of 20,000,000 is useless to him if only a small proportion of it buys the goods advertised. A relatively much smaller audience, of which a high proportion responds to the advertiser's appeal, is obviously preferable.

The soap opera audience, though a fraction of the audience available, has low sales resistance. Its low IQ and many other attributes which, from the standpoint of vigorous democratic health, mark it as a social liability mark it also as the perfect vehicle of sales suggestion. And because "we are selling time for one specific reason . . . to sell goods," a minority of radio's potential daytime audience is made a present, on our two richest networks, of the bulk of daytime sponsored hours.

Free competition of itself, then, does not give us the diversity of programs that we seek and that the advocates of our commercial system theoretically guarantee. Our suggested list of diverse programs remains a list, hardly an item of it adequately represented.

Nor is it feminists alone who are entitled to indignation. The fact that women's interests are slighted is quite incidental — and also accidental to the listening period reviewed. Let the reader check other times of day, and he or she will find a similar monotony, a similar absence of fair coverage of the five program categories we have defined as the people's birthright. Sameness, not diversity, is what we get.[4]

Nor is an absence of diversity our only loss. We — and radio — lose something equally precious, equally essential to a dynamic society. We and radio alike lose the incentive and the scope for writers of talent and imagination to express themselves through the most influential medium of communication that we have. By their shortsighted policy, the networks risk killing the goose that lays the golden eggs. Radio is threatened with sterility. Instead of being the Mecca of all the talents for which radio provides an outlet, it already has some aspects of a ghost town.

It would, of course, be unjust to distinguish between sponsored and sustaining programs as if between good and bad ones. Many sponsored programs are of high standard. Some sustaining ones have very

[4] How large are the minorities of interest now being deprived of what they want is illustrated in a revealing statement by the executive vice-president of CBS, Mr. Paul Kesten. In public hearings before the FCC, in July 1945, he said that 5 per cent of listeners (more than 3,000,000) want good music *all* the time, and less than 10 per cent (he did not say how much less, presumably a fraction), or more than 6,000,000 listeners, want it half the time.

questionable merit. But it remains true that (outside the field of entertainment) sponsored programs, given the present philosophy which informs commercial radio, do not and are not likely to provide us with the diversity that we need. The greater, therefore, the monopoly of program time by sponsored programs, the less the desirable diversity we can look for. This is quite contrary to the classic argument that competition is a spur to richer and more varied service, but it is the conclusion to which we are driven by scrutiny of programs as they are.

How, then, does it come about that so high a proportion of program hours, in each main segment of the day, consists of sponsored material? For it is not the sponsor who receives a license to operate a station, nor is it he who has charge of the policy of our networks. Is the identity of interest of network and of advertising client so close as to eliminate, among the directors of our networks, any feeling of responsibility for public service? At least one network president has answered "Yes" in the quotation cited above. But let us take no man's word for it. Let us again look at some facts.

The networks have always made comfortable profits. But ten years or more ago, business was not as brisk as it is now. The same program hours had to be filled, but for many of them there was no bid from any advertising client. These were the hours filled with sustaining programs, conceived, produced, and financed by the networks themselves. During these hours we heard some of the finest quality programs that have been produced.

Then came the boom era of radio advertising agencies. These were middlemen, go-betweens for the networks and advertisers, who served not only to secure advertising clients for the networks but to think up and produce and provide the casts for the programs sponsored by these clients. The networks were thus enabled to discharge large numbers of their writing and producing staffs, "idea" men and advertising agents, and to sit comfortably back at the receipt of custom, conceding slabs of time, and taking in return the increasingly large sums of money proffered by advertisers for time on the air. The conception and production of programs by the staff of networks became more and more of a marginal operation. Fewer and fewer programs came to us at reasonable hours for which a given network could claim full credit for itself. Either some advertising agency or independent advertiser conceived and produced the program in its entirety, or else the network was, in more or less degree, merely associated with them.

More and more programs are sold, which means that less and less programs stem from the independent initiative of networks or reflect their independent program policy.[5] A graphic chart enables us to see at a glance what would take hours to verify by ear. Look at the charts that follow.

NBC COMMERCIAL AND SUSTAINING PROGRAMS FOR
WEEK BEGINNING DECEMBER 24, 1944, 6:00-11:00 P.M., EWT

EWT - P.M.	SUNDAY	MONDAY	TUESDAY	WEDNESDAY	THURSDAY	FRIDAY	SATURDAY
6:00- 6:15							
6:15- 6:30							
6:30- 6:45							
6:45- 7:00							
7:00- 7:15							
7:15- 7:30							
7:30- 7:45							
7:45- 8:00							
8:00- 8:15							
8:15- 8:30							
8:30- 8:45							
8:45- 9:00							
9:00- 9:15							
9:15- 9:30							
9:30- 9:45							
9:45-10:00							
10:00-10:15							
10:15-10:30							
10:30-10:45							
10:45-11:00							

(Source: NBC Advance Program Service)

Network Commercial Programs

Split Network; part commercial, part sustaining.

Network Sustaining Program.

[5] Recently some "packaged" shows have been produced by networks and sold to sponsors ready-made. But these are still the exception. The typical network commercial program is still largely the product of an advertising agency.

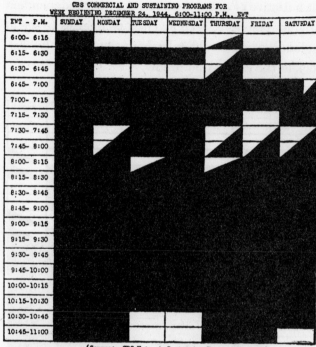

CBS COMMERCIAL AND SUSTAINING PROGRAMS FOR
WEEK BEGINNING DECEMBER 24, 1944, 6:00-11:00 P.M., EWT

(Source: CBS Network Sustaining Program Schedule)

■ Network Commercial Program   □ Network Sustaining Program

◣ Split Network, part commercial, part sustaining

Network spokesmen are tireless in assuring us that they maintain and impose their own policy on the structure and content of programs. Either this is hypocrisy or something very disturbing has come about in the evolution of network policies. Either they reject the principle of diversity of output in the public interest, and have forgotten their own argument

that competition automatically results in such diversity, or they have made a very poor showing in carrying their devotion to the public interest into practice.

The fact is that, with the increasing prestige and
initiative of radio advertising agencies and the increased demands for time on the air by advertisers,
networks have largely abdicated to the interests and
point of view of agencies and firms that have become
more masters than clients. Yet the networks, not the
advertising agencies or their clients — the commercial
sponsors of radio programs — are the recipients of a
public trust. They, not the advertising agencies or
the commercial sponsors, are responsible for the balanced structure of programs, to which the public
is entitled. Without self-restraint and self-regulation, not only are programs fit for a democracy endangered, but the justification of our commercial
system of radio itself comes under question. The in-
toxication of success — success in commerce — has
become delirious. One is reminded of Lord Acton's
warning: "Power corrupts: absolute power corrupts
absolutely." We, the public, must see to it that radio's power, which means primarily the power of
networks, is halted this side of the absolute.

The temptation for networks, admittedly, is very
great. And it is intensified by one ominous aspect
of the advertising picture. The bulk of networks'

advertising revenue comes from a surprisingly small number of advertising clients, and a high percentage of their business is handled by a very small number of advertising agencies. Thus: —

In 1944 26 per cent of CBS business came from four advertisers only.

38 per cent of CBS business was handled by four advertising agencies only.

25 per cent of the Blue Network's business came from four advertisers only.

37 per cent of the Blue Network's business was handled by four advertising agencies only.

23 per cent of Mutual's business came from four advertisers only.

31 per cent of Mutual's business was handled by four advertising agencies only.

The National Broadcasting Company publishes no relevant data.

Or put it another way. In 1944, the gross billings of all networks amounted to $190,677,076. Two types of national advertising business only — drugs and toilet articles (27.9 per cent) and foods and food beverages (22.4 per cent) — provided more than half this revenue.

The reason is obvious. Networks, through their control of affiliated stations, provide an unrivaled, indeed a unique, medium of nationwide advertising. Firms with coast-to-coast business are naturally attracted. Such firms are relatively few in number. Their monopoly of a high percentage of air time, given the conviction that radio advertising pays, is therefore a foregone conclusion.

The consequences may be sinister. If the revenue of networks came from a large and miscellaneous number of advertising clients, the consequences of offending any one of them (in the public interest, for instance) would not be dangerous. Adequate time, reserved for programs in any one of our six categories, could be refused the particular advertiser without fear for the network's over-all continuing prosperity. The length and frequency and quality of advertising copy could be subjected to rules and limitations according to standards set by the network and related to its function as a trustee of the public interest.

But when, as in the case of CBS, 38 per cent of its business is handled by only four agencies and more than a quarter of its business comes from four advertisers, its independence is seriously affected. It would be only human nature if CBS executives, dealing with one of these eight giants, preferred compromise to principle rather than jeopardize or risk the loss of its business.

And compromise must seem all the easier in the absence of any generally recognized standards of what constitutes good programing in the public interest. The Federal Communications Commission has failed, in the eleven years of its history, to define any such elementary standards. And the public, because it has lacked leadership and organized representation, still lacks a bill of rights for radio. There is much discontent, but there is no recognized channel along which it can be directed to secure practical results. Occasionally, letters from individual listeners reach the FCC, complaining of the quality and monotony of programs. The FCC acknowledges receipt and redirects the letter to the station or network complained of. It is not, at present, so constituted as to be able to act promptly, on the people's behalf, on a sufficiency of specific program issues (in such a matter, for example, as the scandal of daytime soap operas).

The networks and stations, beyond certain regulatory principles (such as the FCC's ruling on monopoly respecting the contractual relations between networks and affiliated stations) thus carry the full burden of determining their *own* standards of public service. Certain standards have been defined by the National Association of Broadcasters. But these fall far short of what we have a right to expect.

Like the Ten Commandments, they save us from extreme abuses, but life would be short of our conception of its true possibilities if our moral action were limited to the avoidance of the sins interdicted by the Ten Commandments. Adherence to principle by the networks in their dealings with advertising agencies and advertisers is not, of course, ruled out. It *is* made harder by the situation we have just described, approximating the difficulty of a camel in passing through the eye of a needle.

The profits of our great networks mount steadily. By 1942, the net income of the National Broadcasting Company, after deduction of all expenses and depreciation charges, but before federal income tax, amounted to a return of 137 per cent of its investment. The Columbia Broadcasting System's return was 97 per cent. By 1943, the figures had soared to 190 per cent and 158 per cent for NBC and CBS respectively. Subsequent incomes have been higher still. Yet programs have deteriorated, as many claim, in quality and, as all may see, in their diversity. Networks, succumbing to the lure of profits, have conceded time progressively to advertisers without regard to either quality or program balance. They have abdicated, to an alarming extent, their prime responsibility so to regulate the number and distribution of sponsored programs as to ensure, in each of the three main segments of the day, a diversity of programs sufficient to cover the five main categories hypothetically defined as the listener's due and need in a healthy democracy. That abdication may be regarded, at any rate in part, as due not only to a desire to push profits up to yet more astronomical figures, but also to a fear of giving offense to a small nucleus of advertising agencies and of program sponsors who monopolize a dangerously high percentage of the network's business.

The Fate of the Sustaining Program

The sustaining program is in its nature and function peculiar to our commercial system of broadcasting. It is the complement of the sponsored program. Time has to be filled. If a sponsor is unavailable, a sustaining program must be produced. But it would be a mistake to think of the sustaining program as a mere "residuary legatee" of time not sold. It has distinctive and essential functions to perform.

1. *It is the one means by which a network can impose the stamp of its own will and desire on the overall character and balance of its programs.* Advertisers, as we have seen, tend to select programs mostly from the first two categories in our list of desirable diversified service (news and entertainment). A network

can redress the consequent imbalance in the over-all program structure by originating, and reserving time for, programs in our remaining categories.[6]

2. *It is a means of providing programs which, by their very nature, may not be sponsored with propriety.* Opinions will differ as to what programs should thus be reserved. No one, presumably, would wish to hear the President of the United States sponsored, or the Pope or the King of England. Many are shocked by the sponsorship of religious broadcasts (and may be further shocked to hear that Mutual Broadcasting System's main single source of revenue at one time was payment at commercial rates for religious programs). The radio industry and the public alike appear to be growing less and less sensitive on the subject. Back in 1930 Mr. Merlin H. Aylesworth, the president of NBC said, "I just did not quite like to see the Yale-Harvard game announced 'through the courtesy of so-and-so.'" More recently, in 1941, Mr. Niles Trammell, president of

---

[6] Dr. Frank Stanton, now a vice-president of CBS, described this function to the House Committee on Interstate Commerce on May 7, 1942: "One use Columbia makes of sustaining programs is to supplement commercial offerings in such ways as to achieve, so far as possible, a full and balanced network service. For example, if the commercial programs should be preponderantly musical, Columbia endeavors to restore program balance with drama or the like in its sustaining service."

NBC, listed religious programs, programs by government agencies, and "certain programs involving discussion of political principles and other controversial issues" as "not suited to advertising sponsorship." Children in school, some would contend, should be exempt from the influence of commercial good-will appeals. Times and tastes are deteriorating in this matter but the principle still warrants some defense.

3. *The sustaining program is the only means of catering for minorities that do not appeal to advertisers as a market.* Advertisers want quick returns. They are peculiarly timid pioneers of new program interest. Good music was provided on sustaining time for years before its popularity could be proved to sponsors. Networks have thus to make good the caution and unconcern for anything but quick returns of our rugged individualists.

4. *A corollary of the above is the need for providing sustaining time in which to experiment with new types of program,* unhampered by the restrictive influence of the advertisers' preoccupation with pleasing all and giving offense to none.[7] We are entitled to some peace.

[7] The list of programs first carried as sustainers and subsequently bought by sponsors is a long one. The Metropolitan Opera, the New York Philharmonic Symphony, "Information Please," are but a few examples.

Sustaining programs of course exist, but they have been subject more and more to the slings and arrows of a most outrageous and paradoxical fortune. As the radio industry has prospered the sustainer has lost out. To be specific, sustaining programs are

(1) Far too few to provide the desirable diversity of interest we look for.

(2) Too many of them offered at inconvenient hours.

(3) Too frequently jostled about in time, as sponsors offer to take over the period first allotted to them.

(4) Far too frequently squeezed out altogether as more time gets sold to advertisers for programs not equivalent in type. This, of course, results at once in an unbalanced program structure. Diversity goes by the board.

(5) Far too rarely repeated, for the benefit of listeners who were unavailable at the original (and generally inconvenient) hour of the broadcast.

(6) Far too often rejected by network affiliated stations which substitute local sponsored programs with which to swell their profits. This means that even the relatively few sustaining programs that get on the air are not, in fact, network programs, except in origin, as they

are not rebroadcast by the majority of the network's affiliated stations.

Each of these contentions can be supported statistically. As to the first and second, the reader has only to compare a sample day on any network (or on all four networks together) with the five categories of programs suggested as a yardstick. Or let him turn back to the charts on pages 63 and 64.

Even sustaining programs at inconvenient hours are not safe. Four such, put on by NBC at 11:30 P.M., were reported in *Variety* (May 23, 1945) as going off the air. The four are "Words at War," "Author's Playhouse," "Music for Tonight," and "Music of the New World." *Replacements for each of them, said NBC's program vice-president, would be dance music.* At least one of these, "Words at War," was highly praised and it offered a continuing and all but inexhaustible vehicle for issues and ideas vital to a free democracy.

As to the third and fourth, we have the evidence (supported again and again by similar witnesses during the last ten years) of the executive secretary of the New York Academy of Medicine. "The attitude of the radio stations," he writes, "has been that in giving us time they have discharged their full obligations. Much of the time, incidentally, has been 'small scrap stuff.' It consisted of periods not usually sellable, and our programs have been literally kicked around at the behest of the commercial departments. During the last few months a number of the radio chains and stations have withdrawn the time allotted and have placed us in a position where we have literally to beg for each period. . . . There is another matter which needs to be aired, and that is whether health education should be gauged by the same standards applied to commercial programs, namely, large, mass, popular appeal? There are many items in public health that can only interest a minority of radio listeners. Should the air be barred to us simply because we cannot attract the same size audience that the popular crooners and soap opera programs attract?" [8]

Without conscious irony, an Indiana doctor, speaking at his medical association's annual conference, said this: "For a number of months we have put on programs on a sustaining basis, that is, we do not get a good hour on the radio!"

The reader will himself recall examples of this jostling around of creditable programs, their appearance at one hour during one week, at another a few weeks later, and their sudden disappearance for reasons unconnected with the satisfaction of the audience served. In 1945, striking examples are the demise

[8] Extract from a letter to the FCC quoted at the Wheeler-White hearings, December 1943.

of the "Farm and Home Hour" and the shifting of the "Columbia School of the Air" to after-school hours. The reason given for the latter is that teachers prefer the broadcasts as extracurricular activities. Is it not strange that such a preference should suddenly emerge after broadcasting the program for fifteen years and after the publication of thousands of pamphlets describing and advocating the use of the broadcasts as adjuncts to classroom work?

As to the fifth contention, the failure to rebroadcast fine programs has been a long-standing complaint. When the amount of time and energy devoted to the writing, production, and performance of a good broadcast feature or drama is considered, the waste involved in a single airing seems wanton and stupid. During wartime especially, when thousands of workers on evening and night shifts were unable to hear the main evening broadcasts, failure to repeat at least some of the outstanding performances and commentaries deprived a large body of listeners of the best that radio has to offer. Why this wanton waste?

Now let us look at the facts regarding the coverage given the relatively few sustaining programs which the networks either promote or allow time for. We shall select only such programs as (1) deal with subjects of national interest, or (2) appeal to large and important sections of our national community, and

(3) are widely recognized as being well produced and stimulating. Each of the programs listed below corresponds to one of our six program categories. On every count they seem to deserve the full nationwide coverage which the network system is supposed to provide. What happens in practice? Let us take a sample week in 1944: —

"Invitation to Learning" was a program on CBS in which good books were discussed by a panel of distinguished critics. It was a network offering on the Columbia Broadcasting System and 136 stations were free to carry it. This program was carried by 39 stations.

"The National Radio Pulpit" was a program on NBC of nonsectarian religious interest. Of 179 NBC affiliated stations, 60 carried it.

The "American University of the Air" offered "Lands of the Free," a program on NBC dealing with democracy. Of 114 stations, 24 saw fit to carry this program.

"The Chicago Round Table," judged by many to be the best discussion program on any network, and for successive years actually rated by listeners as the ranking program of its kind, weekly discusses a national or international issue affecting the well-being of everyone. Despite its known popularity, of 84 stations, only 55 carried it.

"Labor for Victory" was a program prepared in

alternation by the CIO and the American Federation
of Labor. At the time under review, it was the only
nationally organized labor program offered on any
network. Of 104 stations, only 35 carried it.

Thus not only are programs in most of our important categories inadequate in number, but the few
we are offered actually reach only a small proportion
of the listening public. The situation has become so
critical that some programs, long established as fa-
vorites with large audiences, have been driven to for-
sake sustaining time and seek a sponsor, not to make
money or even to cover costs, but to secure audience
coverage commensurate with the appeal of the program. Without a sponsor, it is becoming more and
more difficult for an established sustaining program
(let alone a new one) to reach listeners who either
are or may become interested in it.

An outstanding example is that of "America's Town
Meeting." In June 1944, its moderator, George V.
Denny, Jr., broadcast before a studio audience the
announcement that his program would in future be
sponsored by the *Reader's Digest*. The decision to
seek a sponsor was made reluctantly and was evidently unpopular with the studio audience. According to one reporter "there was a mild storm of
hissing." The only reason for the change was the
impossibility of making sure that past audiences

would continue to receive the program regularly. Being a sustaining program, no station owned by, or affiliated with, the Blue Network was required to take it. At least five stations had already discarded it in favor of local sponsored programs that brought in cash, if not credit from the listener. Mr. Denny was afraid that more stations would do the same. The hour occupied by "Town Meeting" represented weekly about $1100 worth of commercial radio time, or $57,200 in a year. The change therefore was all profit to the Blue Network. The only loser was the listener — or at any rate such listeners (and there are many) as object to the sponsorship of such a program.

Thus radio, running in double harness, has been dragged off its true course. The driver has slackened his hands on the reins and let the lead horse of advertising get away with it. The effect on the balance of programs and our diversity of choice has been disastrous. A further consequence, the nuisance of excessive advertising blurbs, we shall examine in a later chapter.

IV

Freedom of Speech on the Air

Eternal hostility against every form of tyranny over the mind of man.

— JEFFERSON

SERGEANT BEN KUROKI, of Hershey, Nebraska, came back from the war. He had been on twenty-nine combat flights in Europe, including the "suicide" raid on the Ploesti oil fields. He wore the Air Medal with four Oak Leaf Clusters.

When he was in Los Angeles . . . a local radio station canceled a broadcast in which he was scheduled to take part on the ground that the appearance of a Japanese-American on a radio program in California would raise a "controversial issue." When he spoke in San Francisco, however, before the Commonwealth Club, he received a ten-minute standing ovation. "I had thought," he said, "that after Ploesti and twenty-nine other missions so rough it was just short of a miracle I got through them, I wouldn't have to fight for acceptance among my own people all over again. In most cases, I don't, and to those few who help breed fascism in America by spreading such prejudice, I can only reply in the words of the Japanese-American creed: 'Although some individuals may discriminate against me, I shall never become bitter or lose faith, for I know that such persons are not representative of the majority of the American people.' The people who wrote that creed are the thousands of Japanese-Americans whom certain groups want deported immediately. These Japanese-Americans have spent their lives proving their loyalty to the United States, as their sons and brothers are proving it now on the bloody battlefields of Italy. It is for them, in the solemn hope that they will be treated justly rather than with hysterical passion, that I speak today." [1]

Thus once again a "controversial issue" became a radio station manager's convenient alibi for avoiding his responsibility, and a plausible excuse for unjust discrimination. It was not the first time this had happened, nor was it to be the last. We propose in this chapter to examine several examples and to discuss the general question of unfair discrimination on the air. What forms does it take? What motive, or what pressure, prompts it?

[1] From *Prejudice*, by Carey McWilliams (Little, Brown & Company, 1944), pp. 287–288. For an exposure of the full measure of our collective guilt, see "Our Worst Wartime Mistake" by E. V. Rostow, September 1945 issue of *Harper's Magazine*.

The nandling of so-called controversial issues presents one of the most perplexing problems faced by radio operators. It is easy to stand aside and criticize. It is quite another matter, as the writer knows from years of personal experience, to solve the problem. What *is* controversial? What constitutes a fair and balanced presentation of a question? How far ahead of public opinion should radio be in blazing the trail towards increased tolerance and enlightenment? How do you select the controversial questions that you raise? What's controversy for anyway? These are only a few of the questions which a responsible radio executive faces every day of his life.

The handling of controversy on the air requires courage, a highly developed sense of social responsibility, and a mature wisdom. Local radio stations have, on the whole, shown a conspicuous lack of these qualities.

Who is responsible to see that news and news comment are "fairly" presented? There has never been any question about that. No matter whether the program is offered in sustaining or sponsored time, the station licensee is answerable. Others — the broadcaster and/or his sponsor — may be held to be accessories, but the station licensee has the primary responsibility.

Next, what constitutes responsibility? There was a

time when some stations abused the privilege of their license to make of radio an instrument for the furtherance of their own particular point of view. This practice was vetoed in a famous FCC decision (the Mayflower decision), part of which is worth quoting. The question arose over the application for renewal of its license by the Yankee Network, Inc. The FCC decision reads, in part, as follows: —

The record shows without contradiction that, beginning early in 1937 and continuing through September 1938, it was the policy of station WAAB to broadcast so-called editorials from time to time urging the election of various candidates for political office or supporting one side or another of various questions in public controversy. . . . It is clear — indeed the station seems to have taken pride in the fact — that the purpose of these editorials was to win public support for some person or view favored by those in control of the station. . . .

Under the American system of broadcasting, it is clear that responsibility for the conduct of a broadcast station must rest initially with the broadcaster. It is equally clear that, *with the limitations in frequencies inherent in the nature of radio,* the public interest can never be served by a dedication of any broadcast facility to the support of his own partisan ends. Radio can serve as an instrument of democracy only when devoted to the communication of information and the exchange of ideas fairly and objectively

presented. A truly free radio cannot be used to advocate the cause of the licensee. . . . *In brief the
broadcaster cannot be advocate.*[2]

The two italicized passages deserve special notice. The broadcaster cannot be an advocate because
of the limitations in frequencies. If he advocates his
own point of view, he abuses a privilege accorded to
him, but withheld from others, because there are not
enough frequencies to go around. If science, which
God forbid, ever makes it possible for all of us to run
a miniature radio station out of our vest pocket, the
Mayflower decision will lapse. A cynical way of putting it would be that in radio we only need to be fair
as long as others haven't an equal chance of being
unfair!

CBS perhaps had the Mayflower decision in mind
when Paul White, its Director of News Broadcasts,
issued what some termed the infamous order of September 1943 to all CBS news analysts. The following
are relevant extracts from this order: —

Columbia has no editorial views. . . . Those men
selected by us to interpret or analyze the news must
also refrain from expression of editorial opinion,
or our non-editorial position becomes an empty shell
. . . we ask you to say to yourselves, "We are not

[2] The Mayflower Broadcasting Corporation — FCC Reports,
Vol. 8, pp. 339–341.

privileged to crusade, to harangue the people or to attempt to sway public opinion. . . ." The function of the news analyst is to marshal the facts on any specific subject and, out of his common or special knowledge, to present these facts so as to inform his listeners rather than persuade them. . . . Freedom of speech on the radio would be menaced if a small group of men, some 30 or 40 news analysts who have nationwide audiences . . . take advantage of their "preferred position" and become pulpiteers.

The great merit of this instruction is that it is binding on *all* news analysts broadcasting over CBS facilities, whether on sustaining or sponsored time. The danger of the sponsor's influence over a news analyst's selection or treatment of his subjects is precluded. CBS honestly and courageously assumes the responsibility that properly belongs to it. Here is a welcome exception to that tendency for a network to abdicate to advertisers and advertising agencies that we noted in the last chapter.

But while we admire the courage and honesty of its intentions, ought we not to question the wisdom of CBS in their interpretation of the Mayflower decision that a "broadcaster cannot be advocate"? Had the instruction applied to news reporters it would have been unchallengeable. Applied to analysts, it seems to overlook the essential purpose of analysis.

What is meant by news analysis? It means, surely,

two things — an explanation of what the news *means*, and an interpretation of what it *signifies*. Russia concludes a pact with China. The different clauses of the pact need explanation. What does it mean, the listener is likely to ask, when it says so-and-so? So far, so good, it would seem, with CBS. "Out of his common or special knowledge" the analyst should be capable of explaining the meaning of a complicated statement without "haranguing" anybody.

But any interested listener is likely to want (and is surely entitled to hear) an interpretation of the significance of the pact. How will it affect Russian relations with the Chinese Communists in Yenan? What does this pact signify to us in America? What is the inside story of its origin? The bare facts of news can be read off a news agency's ticker tape. We tune in to a news analyst because we assume, among other things, that his wider experience and access to more people than we know qualify him to tell us not only what the facts mean but what is their significance.

The analyst's personal sympathies (in the above example for Russia or China) will color his judgment. Boake Carter was consumed with hatred of the country of his birth, England, and with fear and hatred of Russia. Both his selection and his treatment of news out of these countries were colored by his predisposition towards them. Raymond Swing is persuaded that

Russo-American accord is vital to the future peace of the world. That conviction is bound to influence his selection of and emphasis on news that bears on this topic. Should we be debarred from hearing either of these men simply because they have a point of view? What is the use of "common or special knowledge" if it does not contribute to mature, considered judgment? No man has, of course, a monopoly on mature judgment. There is not an analyst on the air who has not at some time judged or guessed wrongly. But, as we shall see, we have other safeguards against witting or unwitting deception of the public than depriving that public of the point of view of any of radio's news analysts. The point of view of an analyst, coupled with his expert knowledge of his subject, is what makes him interesting.

Again, it is surely possible to express an editorial opinion (or, for that matter, to have a sustained editorial point of view) without indulging in "haranguing" or "crusading." This is a question of tone and of emphasis and subject selection. We have some crusaders and haranguers on the air. Fortunately, and to radio's credit, they are the exception, not the rule. The proper way of handling a crusader masquerading as an analyst is either to take him off the air as a news analyst or to assign him other time appropriate to crusades and see to it that others, opposed to his crusading, get equal hearing. (This, of course, involves what may at times prove an embarrassing decision by the network. But responsibility for such decisions is inescapable. It is the price of power.) It is never sound practice to make rules based on exceptional contingencies. CBS has an unequaled record of distinction in the quality and integrity of the news analysts whom it has presented to the public — Edward Murrow, William Shirer, Quincy Howe, to name only a few. These men have not been colorless. They have at times expressed strong and timely points of view. But no one could accuse any one of them of crusading or haranguing. We admire CBS for emulating Caesar's wife. But in an effort to be above suspicion in its analysis of news it has in effect removed itself from the area of suspicion. Caesar's wife has cut and run for it. Instead of the consummation of "the marriage of true minds," divorce proceedings have been instituted!

One final point. Freedom of speech would indeed be menaced "if a small group of men took advantage of their preferred position and became pulpiteers." But here again the fear of an almost inconceivable contingency seems to override common sense. CBS's thirty or forty news analysts show no signs of climbing up into the pulpit. Nor would the noneditorial policy of CBS be threatened if they did — unless they all got into the *same* pulpit. In the Mayflower case the station prided itself on its advocacy of persons and causes. CBS would be in a like case only if it instructed or encouraged all its analysts to advance a point of view of CBS's own choosing.

We have devoted some space to this incident to show how difficult is this whole question of controversy on the air even when approached in a spirit of responsible concern for public interest. It becomes far more complex and serious when possible ulterior motives enter in. The great merit of the CBS's decision was that it precluded any possibility of influence over a news analyst by the sponsor who paid his fee. Is there grounds for believing that such influence exists?

In the November 1943 issue of the *Atlantic Monthly* appeared an article by Quincy Howe, himself a news analyst. "The sponsor," he said, "tends to judge news shows largely on the basis of audience appeal — which in turn puts a premium on sensationalism. . . . The serious news broadcaster . . . finds himself under pressure from two quarters. On the one hand, he is tempted to play up to the widest possible audience; on the other, he is tempted to slant his interpretation the way he thinks his sponsor might like it to go. . . . In recent months we have seen . . . sponsors snap up the news programs with a conservative slant as they never snapped up the programs with a liberal slant. . . . When [the sponsor] buys a news show he will tend, nine times out of ten, to prefer the kind of analyst who at least does no violence to the National Association of Manufacturers. . . . The big wartime profits of American industry and the popular trend away from the New Deal sharpen these conflicts. Sponsors . . . are not only exerting more indirect pressure: the radio public and the news broadcasters . . . are responding to that pressure. . . . Those who take the New Deal line . . . now find they get into trouble with their sponsors."

We do not know on what evidence Mr. Howe bases these claims and he does not, unfortunately, cite any. Some of his statements appear a little sweeping. Audience appeal, for instance, does not necessarily put a premium on sensationalism. Whatever one may think of Mr. Kaltenborn's analyses, no one could describe them as sensational. Yet he has audience appeal.

Again, the news analyst may be tempted to "slant his interpretation the way he thinks his sponsor might like it to go," but it is clear that not all news analysts do so. It would be hard to detect any connection between the National Association of Manufacturers and Raymond Swing. There are clearly significant and numerous exceptions to this rule — if it is one.

Nevertheless Mr. Howe can be presumed to have been writing on the basis of some depressing experiences. This kind of evidence is hard to come by and rarely emerges in a specific form. The techniques of "indirect pressure" are subtle and usually carefully cloaked. If he were alone in his point of view we might discount it as perhaps not representing more than an individual's experience. But others have similar experiences to record.

Mr. Cecil Brown, best known, perhaps, for his description of the fall of Singapore and a reporter and editor of fifteen years' experience, abruptly concluded his broadcast series on September 24, 1943. He was fired. His sponsor was Johns-Manville, one of the twenty largest advertisers on CBS facilities. According to *Variety*, which takes care to check its facts, his contract was canceled because he had advised his listeners to see the movie based on the book *Mission to Moscow*, written by a former U. S. Ambassador to Russia.

Here again we have only reports, and we are unlikely ever to get at the real evidence. We must judge the probability or plausibility of what, it is alleged, transpired by reference to the general context and atmosphere of radio as we have thus far examined it. The Cecil Brown incident sent up a cloud of smoke and there is rarely smoke without a fire. Moreover Cecil Brown's was not the only fire.

Late in June, 1945, a rally was held in Boston, attended by several hundred persons and addressed by Johannes Steel. Mr. Steel had been broadcasting a sponsored commentary on the news on Station WHDH. It was canceled, according to *Variety*, "because of alleged pressure by America First groups. Threats to boycott the Parker Watch Co. [Steel's sponsor], unless the program was dropped, were blamed for the cancellation." Said Mr. Steel: "Your radio stations give you little else but canned goods and have been terrorized by Coughlinite fascist influences into what amounts to a conspiracy of silence on vital issues. I know whereof I speak because I have been broadcasting here for some time and was taken off the air as the result of economic blackmail."

This is strong language and again we have no inside information or substantiated evidence. All we know is that a radio commentator, hitherto apparently respected (or why would a sponsor have chosen him?), had his contract terminated by a sponsor who appears to have acted under pressure. Anyone familiar with Boston politics knows that it requires courage to deal with certain questions considered taboo by strongly organized pressure groups in the locality. But if sponsors are to enter the arena of news analysis may we not ask of them a like courage and fairness to that which we demand of networks and stations in the name of liberty and the First Amendment to the Constitution?

From Station KFI, Los Angeles, reputed to be the most powerful radio station in Southern California, the owner of the station, Mr. Earl C. Anthony, one day penned an identical telegram to each of the six KFI local commentators and their sponsors stating that as of March 1, 1945, news commentaries would be undertaken only by members of the station's own staff. The contracts of all the six commentators would therefore be terminated as from that date. Not one of these men was allowed to broadcast the reasons for his dismissal. It should be noted that the six commentators were not invited to broadcast thereafter on sustaining time. Their contracts were canceled. Others, members of Mr. Anthony's own staff, were to undertake the task. The people of Los Angeles smelt a rat and started in pursuit.

An Emergency Committee was formed and a meeting was held on June 8, 1945, at the Women's Club in Hollywood. The Club's auditorium has seating accommodation for 1500 people and it was filled to capacity. The purpose of the meeting was to protest the action of Station KFI and to collect funds for further action. Collection baskets were passed around and people appeared to be contributing handsomely. Several people made $100 donations and several organizations gave sums amounting to several hundred dollars apiece.

A prominent Los Angeles attorney declared that KFI's news policy meant that, under the guise of impartiality, the station would omit or select news at its discretion, thus exercising, by restraint, a definite editorial policy.

Mr. John B. Hughes, well-known radio news analyst, declared that no news broadcast can be completely impartial, but he believed that a system of independent commentators was better than having all commentary under the control of the station owner. He went on to say that he had had very little trouble with sponsors and that the best of them have never told him what to say. He did, however, admit that one of his contracts was canceled because the sponsor did not want him to talk about postwar planning!

Public opinion was sufficiently aroused for ten California Congressmen to "sign a resolution accusing KFI of censoring news. Letters from angered listeners poured in to the FCC in Washington in such quantities that it had to print special form letters to acknowledge their receipt." [3]

[3] *Los Angeles Daily News*, June 6, 1945.

Regardless of the merits of the case, here is a rare and welcome example of participation by the public, or some part of it, in the discussion of a problem that brings out the crucial relation between radio and democracy.

The four cases we have quoted serve to show the great importance and the real complexity of this question of fair comment. Further examples could be given and wider ramifications illustrated. For instance we have not touched on the question of fair comment as it applies to radio columnists like Walter Winchell and Drew Pearson, whose attacks on individuals and disclosure of inside stories have won for them great audiences and great enemies as well. Whether radio is a proper medium for such traffic is a question well worth pondering, but such broadcasts fall outside the scope of our present inquiry. Winchell and Pearson are not news analysts, whatever alternative title they may care to adopt, and the title should be denied them on the air.

News analysis, as distinguished from news reporting, with which it is often confused (Lowell Thomas reports, he does not analyze news), involves a necessary exercise of judgment. A news analyst must refrain from extreme language and unbridled attacks, on persons or organizations, of a provocative nature unsupported by substantial evidence or unqualified by some equitable reference to the arguments or point of view of those attacked. This is not a curtailment of freedom of speech. Measured language and acknowledgment that other points of view exist are simply part of the good manners of public utterance. Radio communication is, or can be, inflammatory. Violence of any kind is likely to provoke violence. Unless radio is to become simply a platform for charges and countercharges, restraint and a sense of fair play are part of a news analyst's responsibility. There isn't time to provide for endless retaliatory statements by persons and organizations deeming themselves injured parties.

Radio frequencies being limited, no station or network can be advocate. But this does not mean that its news analysts should refrain from expressing points of view — *unless these are dictated by the station or network.*

The virtue of our system of broadcasting is that it offers us safety in numbers. It gives us no assurance of quality. Indeed, given the limited number of men who combine integrity, intelligence, and experience, the general level of analytical ability is likely to be low. Our analysts may include the best; they cannot all be of the best.[4] But safety we do have, as a contrasting situation illustrates.

[4] *Variety* in its July 25, 1945, issue rated twenty-nine of "Radio's Know-it-Alls" as to their qualifications to speak on

For many years the weekly review of events abroad was entrusted in Britain to one person — Vernon Bartlett. Mr. Bartlett was a competent and honest commentator. His reputation among listeners, indeed, was such that he was subsequently elected to Parliament — as some claim, almost entirely on his radio reputation. But, like any commentator worth his salt, he had a point of view, and he expressed it, never obtrusively but with sufficient frequency to provoke increasing resentment among some who did not share his outlook. After many years the BBC discontinued his services. The objection was not to his point of view but to his "preferred position" in giving expression to it on the air. It is inconceivable, even given a similar system of broadcasting, that the American public would have tolerated for so many years a one-man monopoly on exposition of so vital a subject. In this respect, at least, we have a much more alert sense of the dangers of privileged expression and its bearing on democracy than have the British.

But a mere multiplicity of news analysts is not in itself a sufficient safeguard. Even if we assume (which we cannot) a high degree of expert knowledge among all of them, we shall not get fair com-

---

their chosen subject-field. Only three were judged pre-eminently qualified, only three eminently qualified as news analysts.

ment unless two qualifying principles are recognized.

First, a news analyst must argue from premises openly declared. His premises will, or may be, his point of view. We must know it. Neither by innuendo nor by suppression may he distort the facts to suit his point of view.

Nor must he ride a hobbyhorse to death. This will affect his selection of topics. We shall get a partial and lopsided presentation of the facts. We want all the news that we can lay hands on. A news analyst's obsession with one facet of the news must not be allowed to stand between us and the rest of it. Indeed, on matters about which he feels most strongly he will, if he is wise, be the most scrupulous to concede, and within reasonable limits to expound, the opposed point of view. This last is offered as a counsel of perfection, not as a mandatory provision to be imposed on him by the network or station — not, at least, if the second principle of operation is observed.

This second principle is that a network or station must so select its team of analysts as to assure that they represent between them a fair balance of opposed points of view. Only a very broad definition of opposed viewpoints is either possible or desirable. We all know roughly what we mean by a conservative or liberal outlook, even if we disagree in applying either term to any given individual. It is a fair balance of conservative and liberal viewpoints that any team of news analysts should represent. Extremists of the right and left should be excluded from standing teams, for pragmatic reasons. Their point of view is at once so provocative and relatively so unrepresentative as to provoke constant challenge. Extremists are of course entitled to be heard but in time reserved for controversy; they are not entitled to the "preferred position on the air" of regular news analysts.[5]

[5] CBS, in defending its restrictive instruction to news analysts, argued that it was not thereby limiting freedom of speech because "we have set aside regular broadcasting periods in which controversial issues can be and are discussed." This is either disingenuous or extremely naïve. If the judgment or point of view of each and all news analysts is controversial, we have an alarmingly broad definition of controversy and must make correspondingly broad and ample provision for it on the air. As we shall argue later, the present scope for controversial discussion seems to us to be too limited. But if we accept CBS's implied conception of what is controversial the present scope is utterly inadequate. CBS indeed hasn't time enough at its disposal to provide for the controversy we now must have. Any man who opens his mouth before a microphone to utter an opinion must, on this basis, be answered. This is carrying controversy to ridiculous and impracticable extremes. Conservative and liberal opinion in America is sufficiently evenly balanced to warrant its expression in general without challenge or rebuttal — as long as the two points of view are fairly balanced in the over-all provision for them among news analysts collectively. Time for controversy can then be left to the balanced representation of extreme views and/or to selected issues on which conservatives and liberals feel particularly strongly, which are unlikely to pass without a clamor arising for their rebuttal.

Variety, in its issue of July 25, 1945, published its appraisal of thirty radio reporters and analysts, listing their education, experience, and distinctions, and estimating their "political slant." Twelve of those listed were judged to be conservative (five of them being described as reactionaries or extreme reactionaries); eight were dubbed liberal (most of them "middle-of-the-road" liberals; one only "independently liberal"; none extreme liberals); six were defined as "middle-of-the-roaders"; four defied classification. Even if we accept, as some will not, a ratio of 12:8 as representing the ratio of conservative and liberal thought throughout the country, a fair over-all balance is not achieved if five of twelve conservatives are reactionaries or extreme reactionaries, while the majority of liberals are middle-of-the-roaders and not one very liberal or extreme liberal is represented. The over-all balance is unfairly weighted on the conservative side.[6] True, some conservatives dub all lib-

---

[6] During the last Presidential campaign, according to a seven weeks' survey by the Political Action Committee of thirty-three network programs of news and comment, one broadcaster, Morgan Beatty, quoted antilabor as opposed to prolabor opinion in a ratio of about twelve items to one. In all programs "The PAC uses coercive tactics" was the most frequent theme presented. "The PAC is communist linked" ranked second. Upward revision of the Little Steel Formula was called "dangerous and inflationary" twice as often as it was said to be "necessary due to the rise in prices."

erals as reds. This may be good politics but it isn't good sense.

This leads to the consideration of whether sponsorship exerts an undesirable, because undemocratic, influence on the selection of balanced teams of news analysts. To abolish such sponsorship is unthinkable. Some control over the influence of sponsors, however, is, up to a point, practicable and, on the evidence, does seem desirable.

The experience of Quincy Howe, Johannes Steel, John Hughes, and Cecil Brown, to cite only the cases we have reviewed, suggests that some sponsors tend to influence news analysts regarding the subjects they treat and the way they treat them. This is an unwarrantable interference with free speech. Any sponsor's interest is, or should be, limited to securing an audience for the sales talk which accompanies the program that he sponsors. That audience is in general assured him from the start in that most sponsors take over a news analyst who has already proved his power to attract an audience on sustaining time. By taking him over, the sponsor secures that audience and, if he so desires, secures also an analyst whose political slant he approves.

He may of course take over a news analyst whose views he disapproves of *because* of the audience to which he thereby secures access. But he does this at his own risk. He is not entitled, after the event, to tell him what to say or what subject not to touch. This is to trespass on ground reserved to the network or station in question, which is responsible for putting a balanced team on the air.

No rules or regulations can stop up every loophole against the exertion of influence or indirect pressure. In all human affairs we must rely ultimately on decency and fair play. But much is at stake here and some improvement in our present situation seems feasible to protect the listener against possible abuses of which he, after all, is the final victim. We offer the following suggestions: —

Every contract between a news analyst and his sponsor should contain a clause reserving to the former full responsibility, within the law, for what he talks about and how he talks about it.

No sponsor should be allowed to cancel a contract (termination is another matter altogether) without the knowledge and consent of the station or network in question where the point at issue is the tone or content of the script. The station's or network's interests are involved, a given news analyst being a member of a team which the station or network is responsible for keeping in balance.

The team should be kept in balance, *irrespective of the question of sponsorship.* One way of doing this would be the adoption, for news analysts, of an excellent practice originated by CBS, namely the preparation of "package" programs. These programs are planned and produced by the network and their time fixed. Program and time are then made available for purchase by a sponsor, but all control over the program is reserved to the network. If the whole team of news analysts were thus made available to sponsors in the form of package programs, with "all rights reserved," proper balance and, as far as is humanly possible, a safeguard against influence by sponsors would be secured. Members of the balanced team would be present on sustaining time, as part of the network's public service.

The practice of sponsorship would be less objectionable if sponsors included associations not identified with big employer interests. Unfortunately, until August 1945 the code of the National Association of Broadcasters (of which two thirds of radio stations are members) specifically precluded sponsorship by one important and powerful interest group — labor. This brings us to the second aspect of the problem of controversy which radio illustrates — the question of unfair discrimination.

DISCRIMINATION ON THE AIR

Anyone who has held a responsible position in radio knows the embarrassment, and sometimes the real difficulty, of saying "no" to people. There is always someone knocking at your door, eager to come in and sell you a bright idea, to plead for a worthy cause. Politicians can always do with a little free time to keep their name before the public. Earnest educators propound plans for intolerably tedious talks. A radio executive has to acquire the art of refusing with a smile, the tactics of delayed action, the argument of prior commitment. There isn't time for everybody, and he knows it. His program chart is filled without an effort. His continuing problem is the excess of legitimate demands of public interest over his power to supply. He constitutes a one-man court of arbitration trying to figure out fair allocation of priorities of need.

One yardstick of priority of need is the known size of audiences likely to be interested. Evidence of the public's desire to hear is the best answer to the crank and the logroller who evidences only a desire to be heard. Unfortunately radio has too often disregarded clear evidence of need and interest. The needs and interests of labor organizations are a case in point.

In 1939 membership of labor unions totaled some

13 millions. Together with their families, these union members represented nearly 40 per cent of the American public. They shared a common interest in union matters and, many of them, a common point of view on a number of social, economic, and political questions besides. Yet in 1944 "Labor for Victory" was the only nationwide program on the air representing labor interests.[7]

Nor is this all. Before the Senate Committee on Interstate Commerce the CIO has cited more than a dozen cases of what it regarded as unfair discrimination against labor. The cause and the consequences of this discrimination need to be examined.

The immediate cause is a provision in the code of the National Association of Broadcasters which is worth quoting in full: —

> Time for the presentation of controversial issues shall not be sold, except for political broadcasts. There are three fundamental reasons for this refusal to sell time for public discussion and, in its stead, providing for it without charge. First, it is a public duty of broadcasters to bring such discussion to the radio audience regardless of the willingness of others to pay for it. Second, should time be sold for the discussion of controversial issues, it would have to be

[7] "Nationwide" is a misnomer. For reasons we have examined earlier, of 104 stations which might have carried this program, only 35 did.

sold, in fairness, to all with the ability and desire to buy at any given time. Consequently all possibility for regulating the amount of discussion on the air in proportion to other elements of properly balanced programing or of allotting the available periods without regard to listener interest in the topics to be discussed would be surrendered. Third, and by far the most important, should time be sold for the discussion of controversial public issues and for the propagation of the views of individuals or groups, a powerful public forum would inevitably gravitate almost wholly into the hands of those with the greater means to buy it.

This ruling places responsibility squarely on the shoulder of stations and networks to "bring such discussion to the radio audience as a public duty." It implies, too, that stations and networks define for themselves what constitutes a controversial issue. But read further in the NAB manual and you will discover that this is not so.

"Discussion (or dramatization) of labor programs on the air *is almost always of a controversial nature.* Even the so-called 'facts' [*sic*] about labor . . . are usually challenged." One wonders why, but the NAB leaves nothing to the imagination. It gives stations and networks a persuasive tip-off — an appeal to the pocketbook — as to why they will do well to observe the code. "Employers as a whole won't discuss their labor problems on the air and *are inclined to frown on those stations, especially in smaller communities, which open their facilities to labor leaders."* Radio station managers, in other words, especially the little men "in smaller communities," risk a boycott on advertising revenue if they perform their "public duty" to nearly 40 per cent of the American public. The argument goes further than a concern with program balance and the unfairness of putting controversy up to auction. It reaches out, by implication, to sustaining time as well. Discuss labor at all and you'll lose your only source of livelihood.

Networks and stations, with a few honorable exceptions, have not been slow to respond to this crack of the whip, as a few examples (many more could be cited) will show.

Let us hear first the testimony of a former president of the Blue Network, Mr. Mark Woods. Appearing before the Federal Communications Commission in 1943, he thus answered questions put to him: —

QUESTION. Now suppose the A.F. of L. wants . . . to come on with a general program to build up good will for the A.F. of L., would you sell them time?

WITNESS. We should not sell time to them.

QUESTION. Suppose General Motors comes along and

says "We want to put on a program and
we will use Vandercook as a commentator and also that this program is
brought to you by the courtesy of General Motors," would you sell time for
that?

WITNESS.   Yes, we would.

QUESTION.   Suppose the A.F. of L. came along and
said that they wanted to put a program
on and wanted to have Vandercook as the
commentator too, how would you handle
that?

WITNESS.   No, we won't sell time to the A.F. of L.

QUESTION.   . . . You still would not sell the A.F. of
L. time for a symphony program?

WITNESS.   That is correct, Mr. Chairman.[8]

Or take an example from a local station. In San
Francisco the CIO succeeded in securing a daily sustaining program in which for two years it broadcast
CIO news over Station KYA. But then the contract
was terminated, with a reference to the NAB code
provisions. Despite this, "large corporations in the
same area," according to sworn testimony by a CIO
representative, "continued to subsidize news and
amusement programs, a number of which evidence a
bias in favor of the employer corporation."

[8] Following a courageous stand on this issue by the then
chairman of the FCC, James Lawrence Fly, the Blue Network changed its policy in this matter.

But perhaps the most flagrant example of prejudiced discrimination occurred in New York. During the 1944 elections, the Greater New York Industrial Council sought time on various New York stations for spot announcements urging listeners to register. No one was asked to vote for any party. No candidate or party was even referred to. Yet six stations refused to accept these announcements.

It might be argued that sponsors have no business associating their names with civic causes — in this case the supreme responsibility of a citizen of a democracy to record his vote. But radio is in no position to advance this argument. For three years it has permitted commercial sponsors to win good will for themselves by sponsoring appeals to patriotism and self-sacrifice necessitated by the war. An appeal to vote is every bit as important as an appeal to subscribe to the Red Cross. Yet Labor was denied the right to make this appeal.

This whole problem of discrimination has been dragging on for years. It came to a head in 1943 when the CIO took up the case of Station WHKC, Columbus, Ohio. Columbus has a population of about 306,000. CIO members in the city together with their families number about 120,000.

The CIO petitioned the FCC not to renew the license of this station on the grounds of "improper,

unfair and discriminatory action." Specifically it
claimed that scripts by CIO members had been censored in a way both to limit fair comment and even
to distort the speaker's point of view. Indeed the
"censorship became so intolerable that the petition-
ers found themselves forced to cancel the 52-week
contract with WHKC altogether."

Limitation of a speaker's right to comment does not
in itself involve discrimination. Discrimination enters in only when others are not subject to the same
restrictions. The CIO testimony before the FCC cited
instance after instance of license accorded to others
to air their opinions, while the CIO was kept in
leading strings.

It singled out for special condemnation three commentators — Boake Carter, Upton Close, and Fulton
Lewis. While the CIO was censored — for example,
in what it said about housing in the hands of specu-
lative builders — Fulton Lewis was allowed to spring
to their defense and to abuse government housing
projects in terms that provoked the following letter
from the head of the National Housing Agency:
"Your various broadcasts on housing on your present
trip have given an unfair and distorted picture and
repeatedly confused war housing with the prewar
low rent and slum clearance."

Fulton Lewis has been criticized by many others

for his violent and hostile tirades on many public issues and even against public figures. He once went the length of accusing the Truman Committee of being responsible for lowering aircraft production. On another occasion scores of telegrams were received from the West Coast by the FCC charging that he had libeled the Screen Office Members' Guild. In a letter to the editor of *In Fact* he admitted to having been in the pay of the National Association of Manufacturers until June 1942.

If our suggested principles applicable to news analysis were adopted, and if the complaints about him were substantiated, Fulton Lewis would now be off the air as violating the principle of restraint and of an open declaration of his premises. But this is not the issue pertinent to our present argument. The witnesses of the CIO in sworn testimony placed in parallel columns scripts by their speakers, heavily censored, and scripts by Fulton Lewis, Boake Carter, and Upton Close, uncensored and containing one-sided and arbitrary opinions on subjects identical with those discussed by their own representatives. These speakers, moreover, were dealing in controversy on paid-for time, a violation of the NAB code which, rightly or wrongly, does not exempt commentators. This is discrimination.

But the discrimination goes further. Even on sus-

taining time balanced controversy does not obtain.
Here, too, the employer receives preferred consideration, for employers, as potential patrons of sponsored
programs, "are inclined to frown on those stations
. . . which open their facilities to labor leaders." In
addition to sponsored time the employer gets a
generous slice of sustaining time in which to advance his point of view, as the following example
shows.

For many years the National Association of Manufacturers has been active on the air. As long as ten
years ago it had recognized the power of radio to
sway public opinion.[9] It was vigorous in its denunci-
ation of the Wagner Act in 1935, claiming, on Station WOR, that "it would prolong the depression,
increase industrial unrest . . . and ultimately place
the control of American industry and labor under
the domination of the A.F. of L." Another of its
speakers, over a nationwide network, asked, "How
can sensible men talk of equality of bargaining power
between responsible employers and irresponsible labor organizations?"

In a pamphlet issued by its Information Committee
in 1937 it boasted that "for three years the NAM
has been developing its carefully conceived program

[9] "Now more than ever," it claimed in a pamphlet widely
circulated to its members, "strikes are being won or lost in
the newspapers and over the radio."

of public information. . . . Day after day, systematically and forcefully, this program hammers home . . . the facts about American industry." Such "facts," we must remember, include the claim (which time does not appear to have substantiated) that passage of the Wagner Act would "place the control of American industry . . . under the domination of the A.F. of L." and blanket assumptions that labor organizations are "irresponsible."

For such fact finding radio has provided free time, time which, according to the 1937 president of the Association, "would cost a million dollars to buy." The most widely circulated program of the Association is the "American Family Robinson." "There are over 250 transcriptions in this series and they have been broadcast weekly and semi-weekly over 258 stations." Typical of the "facts" thus presented is the following extract from one of these transcriptions. The hero of the drama speaks: —

It is true that some European countries do have social security laws — but you can't name one whose system works better than the one we have right here in America. They need them. Here, workmen for 150 years have enjoyed security of wages and working conditions that enable them to provide homes, education, insurance, and other benefits for themselves and their families. . . . But you can't get security just by passing a law. You have to provide money for it — and there's only one place that money can come from — payroll taxes — which means lower wages.

This is no statement of facts but a provocative advancement of a biased point of view. It is propaganda, veiled as exposition.

The full extent of this Association's efforts to influence the public is revealed in the following figures. "Since December 3, 1934, the Association . . . prepared and distributed between 16,777 and 17,500 electrically transcribed records for the use of radio stations."

Labor, debarred from the purchase of time on the air, because "even the so-called facts about labor are usually challenged," received no comparable allotment of sustaining time.

Impressed by such facts, FCC Commissioner Ray Wakefield, considering the case of Station WHKC, wrote an important decision with which the entire Commission concurred. He concluded that any ban on the sale of time for the discussion of controversial issues was not in the public interest. Two months later, the NAB itself revised its code to eliminate a ban which, as we have seen, involved unwarranted and arbitrary discrimination against a large section of the listening public.

Discrimination against labor is probably the most

flagrant example of abuse by radio stations of their privileged position. But it is not the only one. The co-operative movement has likewise had to struggle for admission. Negro artists have frequently been boycotted in deference to Southern prejudices. Indeed the Negro case has gone largely unheard, though CBS has followed an enlightened and enlightening policy in occasional programs that have confronted us with an unanswerable challenge to our consciences. Slowly the area of discrimination is being narrowed, but always by protest, by costly and prolonged petitions. The radio industry responds ultimately to pressure but it is unfortunate, both for its own good name and for the growth of radio as an invigorating social influence, that the course of progress should be thus strewn with obstructions on the way. Even without gratuitous discrimination the problem of controversy on the air is hard enough to solve. Given a greater measure of integrity, a higher degree of courage, and a fuller sense of social responsibility, we could, and should, have the greatest sympathy with men facing a really complex problem. Even where, as in round tables and forums, proponents of opposed points of view participate in balanced controversy, the problem of equity and of public advantage is not easily solved. This is the third of the main issues which we have undertaken to consider.

Discussions on the Air

The most widely publicized of our radio discussion programs is, perhaps, "America's Town Meeting." Its title is well chosen to evoke memories and associations with one of America's most distinctive democratic institutions. The town meeting of old times survives only in a few country townships. Radio has sought to preserve its function on the air. Does it and can it? It is without any desire to disparage this program that we raise the question. We raise it, rather, to bring out the difficulty inherent in all radio discussion.

What characterized the town meetings of earlier times? For one thing, most members of the community participated. They were present and each said his piece if he wanted to. For another, each and all knew the subject. The questions discussed were local questions touching the lives and interests of those present in very immediate and concrete ways. And, thirdly, the meeting came to decisions. Those present spoke their piece and cast their vote.

Discussion on the air is different. The audience is, inevitably, a small section of the national or local community. The listener does not, because he cannot, say his piece. The issues are not local, in a physical sense, even though they touch the audience, if not as immediately at any rate as vitally as the old town hall questions. Nor is any decision come to.

This, then, is a very different occasion and environment. It is a modern attempt to solve a modern problem — how to give individuals a feeling of group participation in the solution of questions very relevant to each of them, but increasingly varied, complex, and remote in their context. All this raises some fascinating and baffling questions of radio technique.

What benefit we derive, as listeners, from radio discussions is materially affected by two main factors — the factor of time and the factor of tone. Time on the air is a pitiless tyrant. Listening to a person whom you cannot see involves strain. It can be demonstrated scientifically that, as time passes, listener attention flags. Listening to a half hour of closely reasoned argument carries us to the limit of sustained attention. This has some very disconcerting consequences. Consider a few. (*a*) Even the simplest of questions cannot be exhaustively discussed in half an hour. Any conclusion we come to, therefore, will be based on partial evidence and incompletely developed reasoning. (*b*) The old town meeting discussed matters familiar to all present. Radio discussion is generally concerned with questions which involve not only exhaustive examination but prior explanation. It is useless, for instance, to discuss the

future of India without first communicating some of
the essential facts about India's past and present.
There are quite a lot of such facts. A great many
people hold confident opinions about India com-
pounded of strong sentiment and gross ignorance.
How can you combine in half an hour a sufficiency
of fact with a sufficiency of reasoned argument based
on facts? (*c*) In half an hour you cannot present more
than a very limited number of speakers if each is to
have time enough to say anything worth while. And
here again listening "blind" contributes to your
troubles. Even with skilled production it is difficult
for the listener to keep more than three or at the
most four speakers clearly identified. This becomes
virtually impossible in free discussion where any
speaker interrupts another at will.

Consider, next, the question of tone. Controversy
can serve several purposes. Like the old Roman gladi-
ator contests, it can be used to put on an exciting
show. One radio discussion program, emanating from
Washington, performs this function admirably. We
get, every Monday evening, a verbal all-in wrestling
match in which you continuously hear the thud of
one or other of the contestants as, caught in a half
nelson, he is thrown out of the ring. Perhaps it matters little that the wrestlers are frequently the people's representatives in Congress displayed stripped

to the waist and divested of all restraint and dignity, and that the ring is the great arena of our national and international interests and obligations.

Debate (as represented by "America's Town Meeting") is another form of controversy. This, too, tends to be a wrestling match, but not of the all-in variety. There are rules and restraints, but the atmosphere of contest is there. Men "argue for victory," as Dr. Johnson put it. Views are expressed in concise, dogmatic terms. There is sharp rejoinder. An occasional rotten egg is thrown in by members of the audience. Tension and partisanship seem to be aimed at. The air is electric.

Or controversy can be used to generate, not heat, but light. Lyman Bryson's program and the "Chicago Round Table" exemplify this objective. The pace here is slower, the atmosphere friendlier. While opposed views are expressed, one is conscious of an effort to reconcile differences or, if this is obviously impossible, to make clear the grounds of difference. Though we may remain unconvinced we may yet learn to respect and understand the other fellow's point of view.

Public reaction to these variant uses of controversy is instructive as it illustrates what the listening public is in search of when it tunes in to controversy, and as it also illustrates the radio producer's success in tackling the twofold problem of time and tone. For many years the largest audience (amounting to several million listeners) has been consistently attracted to the "Chicago Round Table." The smallest audience for the four programs referred to is that for the all-in wrestlers. This seems at once a tribute to the intelligence of the public and an indication of how crucial in radio discussion is the mastery of techniques appropriate to the medium. No discussion program on the air results from greater attention to the technical, as well as intellectual, problems raised in radio communication than the "Chicago Round Table." As far as tone goes, it would seem that what the "Chicago Round Table" loses in excitement (some critics say it is too academic) it gains in interest. The inexorable claims of limited time are met by meticulous preparation in advance. The speakers are limited in number to a normal maximum of three or four. Each receives, well in advance, a carefully prepared digest of the subject to be discussed (pertinent data, statistics, and publications on the subject are summarized). The speakers meet a day or two previous to the broadcast to exchange their opinions. From this exchange their salient points of difference emerge and a limited few are selected as their agenda on the air. On the day of the broadcast and immediately before "air time," the speakers meet in the studio and from brief notes engage in ad lib discussion. This discussion, constituting a dress rehearsal, is recorded and the record is then played back to the speakers. (There is no surer means of convincing a man of defects in his performance than to have him listen to his own voice.) The speakers, advised by the producer, take note of roughnesses and obscurities in the record and, with these fresh in mind, proceed to the actual broadcast. During the broadcast, if a speaker tends to monopolize the time, to interrupt too much, to say too little, a card is placed before him by the producer with an instruction in clear print calculated to correct his defect. Thus while a maximum spontaneity is secured (there is no reading from a manuscript) a minimum of wastage of precious time is likewise provided for. While far from perfect, this program represents (as listeners' reaction would seem to indicate) the best solution yet of the complex problems of discussion on the air.

But no one of the four programs we have mentioned is, or perhaps can be, free from one serious defect resulting from the tyranny of time. The subjects discussed are almost invariably too vast for any but the most superficial treatment. All suffer from the danger of reducing complex questions to a barbarous simplicity. Probably we need a supplementary technique to make good this defect. Discussions would be more fruitful of understanding and of sober judgment if they climaxed lengthier exposition of the subject. A discussion on India, for instance, would be the more useful if it had been preceded by a symposium, or talks series, in which facts and points of view had been aired at greater length. In international affairs particularly our views too often rest on prejudice and sentiment unsupported by knowledge of the facts. Our education has not kept pace with the rapid shrinking of the globe and the terrifying expansion of knowledge. We know less and less about more and more. The only answer to the dilemma is to increase our store of knowledge. Discussion is one means of thus increasing knowledge through the stimulus of hearing opposed points of view based on evidence offered to us. No country in the world probably has as much discussion on the air as we have. But the question remains — have we enough to meet our needs?

Opinions will differ as to how much "enough" amounts to. Since our concern is with the future well-being of democracy, we choose a democratic yardstick to measure by. In any democracy decision on great issues rests finally on the consent of the people. Both information and discussion on the air should at least be sufficient to keep people abreast of these issues. This is only a small segment of the total area in which many-sided discussion can usefully take place, but it might suffice. Given this measure of sufficiency are we well served? No up-to-date research on the subject is available, but in 1941 a survey was undertaken which throws some light on the question.

In early 1941 the country faced tremendous issues. We had already set foot on the steppingstones that led to war. Should we step onward or withdraw? This question then presented itself in terms of decision on certain concrete steps about to be taken. Five major issues of foreign policy confronted us — Lend-Lease, convoys to Britain, the acquisition of foreign bases and foreign ships, and the maintenance of the British blockade. The passage of time will have already dimmed many people's memory of the strong feelings, pro and con, entertained on these questions only five years back. They were strongly felt and strongly expressed. The period of controversy continued from January through May. To what extent did radio reflect, in terms of balanced controversy, the tension of the times?

Networks and stations were invited by the FCC to submit scripts, broadcast during this five-month period, that bore on any one of these five main issues of our foreign policy. Scrutiny of the scripts judged relevant showed that each network broadcast a program on one or other of these subjects every third day.

But while the networks made these programs available, only a fraction of their affiliated stations carried them. Thus, of 120 CBS affiliates 59.3 per cent only carried the average Lend-Lease program. Of 105 Mutual stations 45.5 per cent carried it. Of the many stations on the combined Red and Blue Networks then controlled by NBC 69 only carried the average NBC program on Lend-Lease. A listener would have had to listen, on the average, for nearly ten days to hear one Lend-Lease program of network origin.

Listeners fared far worse in programs not of network origin. Of 842 stations then on the air only 388 claimed to have originated even one program on any of the five foreign-policy questions. And 454 stations ignored all five subjects altogether.

Networks, we might say, made an honest, if not superlative, effort to face up to the crisis. Their affiliates invalidated this effort by extensive nonparticipation and failed to compensate by any effort of their own. It seems almost inconceivable in retrospect that more than half the stations in the country should have done nothing to relate these great issues to the lives and interests of their several communities. But so reads the record of five years ago.

Our current situation is roughly this. Each of four networks offers us regular weekly discussion of some national or international problem. (But these programs reach only a fraction of the audiences that might like to hear them because so many network affiliates choose not to carry them.) From time to time Congressmen and others also express their points of view in sequent talks on particularly burning topical questions. The large majority of local stations make little or no effort to promote discussion at the local level. Over these stations controversy, except as piped in from the networks, is almost extinct. This at a time when more issues of greater complexity at the local, regional, and national levels confront us than at any time in our history. It hardly seems enough.

What, then, do we conclude would be a healthier situation? First, at the network level we might reasonably ask for more than the present provision of time for discussion. Provision of one discussion period a week, on each of four networks, hardly measures up to the claims on our attention represented by the vital issues that confront us in the postwar world.

Second, it would seem reasonable to ask that more consideration be given to the practicable limits of useful discussion dictated by the complexity of subject matter. Too often questions are raised for which no adequate background of knowledge exists in the listener's mind. There are genuine dangers to intelligent appreciation of the issues involved by reducing vast subjects to what we term barbarous simplicity. We might do well to chew off less at a time and nibble more frequently. The technique of explanatory talks series preceding discussion has been suggested as one means of overcoming the inevitable limitations of time for radio discussion.

Third, we might ask that more serious thought and greater trouble be devoted to the techniques of presentation. We have tried to illustrate how vitally these may affect both the interest aroused and the attitude or state of mind of the listener that is induced. On domestic issues of controversy particularly, while a dogfight may be good entertainment, it is almost certain to provoke more heat than light. Given the tensions that exist in our society, is it wise to present contestants as prize fighters or to convey the impression of interests arrayed in battle order? Good temper and a respect for other points of view are part of the good manners of public discussion which seem worth cultivating.

Fourth, at the local station level, we can surely ask for a vast extension of time devoted to discussion and balanced controversy. If what was said, in the chapter on local stations, of the importance of feeding the grass roots of our society is in any degree true, the local station has a unique responsibility and opportunity. The opportunity is twofold — to increase social solidarity within communities by bringing tension and difference out into the open, and to relate national and global issues, in relevant terms, to the immediate interests and environment of the local listener. Over local stations the chances are far greater of achieving a modern counterpart of the old town meetings. A fuller sense of participation (because of greater knowledge and a more immediate sense of the relevance of local issues raised) can be achieved. At the local level, too, radio discussion has a far better chance of resulting in actual decisions. Local radio stations might easily become the most vital influence in a community for harmony and cooperative action.

We are all too conscious that we ourselves are guilty of having, in this survey, bitten off more than we can chew. But the attempt will have been worth while if it has heightened our sense of the fundamental principles at stake here. It is time to sum up and state a broad conclusion.

Freedom of speech over the air is a vital contemporary issue for two reasons — the continuing danger (yes, even in America) of some degree of thought control, and the great opportunity which radio offers us to achieve, at last, an intelligent and well-informed electorate. In radio we thus see illustrated the integral relation between danger and opportunity on which preoccupation with the cause of freedom centers. Let us clarify this relation.

When we speak of wanting freedom we express a twofold desire. One desire is negative and quite specific — to be rid of an undesired restraint. The other is positive and less specific — a desire to *achieve* something which previous restraint has interdicted. We are seldom clear as to what that something is, but always there lurks in the concept of freedom (often as an illusion, a mere will-o'-the-wisp) the vague but potent hope of some fulfillment beyond the mere removal of restraints. In radio, as in any other context where freedom is concerned, it is easier, and far more important, to be clear and of one mind about the restraints in which we see danger to ourselves than to define specific benefits, beyond emancipation from restraint, that we aspire to. We must, moreover, identify not only the danger but its source if we are to eradicate it. In concluding our survey of freedom on the air, let us begin, then, by identifying the danger and its source.

We are immediately confronted with a paradox which has deluded many into a false sense of security. For centuries the horizons of men's knowledge have been limited by poor means of communication. Journeys of the mind, if not of the imagination, have, like travel, been restricted. Now, with books, papers, magazines, and radio, the flood of verbal communication threatens to drown us. But have we, thereby, achieved *freedom* of the mind? Is true knowledge more accessible than it was over fifty years ago? Consider these facts.

At the beginning of this century the population of America was less than 80 million. Now it exceeds 130 million. In 1900 the number of daily newspapers was 2350, but today it is only 1850. Moreover not only has the number of our daily newspapers gone down but so has the number of independent publishers. Chain development is not confined to stores. Newspaper chains today predominate. Even in as great and proud a city as San Francisco one newspaper has the doubtful privilege of calling itself "the only home owned newspaper." The great majority of American towns have no paper that isn't owned and operated by a chain. Similar empires have grown up in the magazine world. More and more people read, but what they read is dictated by fewer and fewer people.

Radio, while it provides a new and independent outlet, is, as we have seen, subject to the same centripetal tendency. Radio began as a conglomerate of

independent local stations. Today their independence
and initiative have, to a serious extent, been ceded
to the networks. Nor is radio as independent an outlet as some suppose. One third of our radio stations
are owned by various press interests.[10]

Thus, while the supply of verbal and written communication has expanded enormously, control over
the media of communication has become progressively restricted. Herein lies the paradox. While food
for thought was never more abundant, nor the means
of distribution more plentiful, we face the prospect
of an "ever shrinking marketplace of thought." Here
is the source of danger — the concentration of power.
The danger itself is a restraint, resulting from abuse
of power, in the most precious of all markets.

We have tried to illustrate how such restraints may
come about and what curtailment of freedom they
may induce. We have suggested some remedies, left
some questions to the reader to mull over. The whole
problem defies brief analysis. Where freedom is concerned equity cannot be reduced to nice arithmetic.
Two and two do not make four. A speaker at six

---

[10] Some of the worst cases of discrimination have occurred
on stations owned by newspaper proprietors who thus man-
age to impose editorial censorship in some communities on
press and radio alike. The FCC at one time had this matter
of joint press-radio ownership under critical review, but
came to no decision. The problem, a nice one, and the potential danger, a real one, are with us still.

o'clock on Monday is answered by his opponent at nine on Thursday. The audience is not the same nor is there a guarantee that the second speaker will even debate the same points. (Witness the farcical duel in 1945 between Walter Winchell and Martin Dies.) But a speaker, engaging in high controversy, and unanswered before any audience at any time, provokes at once a sense of gross injustice. Thus we exact, as one might say, symbolic justice, a token payment to our sense of fair play.

Again, all sides of any question are never heard in radio discussion programs. We are satisfied with a "fair" balance of opinion. Again what we look for is approximation to real equity. In human affairs it is rarely possible to look for more.

Indeed such is our present state that we can confidently leave such niceties to a more utopian future. We still have a more elementary justice to fight for. Our concern is still with the elimination of restraints that are an open defiance of our civil rights. Our business, as listeners, is to keep an eye on the abuse of power by radio's quasi-monopolists. Radio's concern is to keep the public conscience at the quick and its intelligence from atrophy. As Justice Black has said, "The authors of the first amendment knew that novel and unconventional ideas might disturb the complacent, but they chose to encourage a free-

dom which they believed essential if vigorous enlightenment was ever to triumph over slothful ignorance." [11]

The fruits of controversy, in terms of enlightenment or adjustment of outlook, are of course of slow
growth. A revealing book, which has received far
less attention than its due,[12] gives us a salutary re-
minder of how ingrained is prejudice and how pre-
determined (by environment, age, wealth, and so on)
are many of our points of view. But not all our judgments are custom bound. There are many subjects
in which our interest is still unawakened and our
opinion uncrystallized. It is on such that the expression of divergent opinion is likely to be most fruitful
of enlightenment. And, ignorance being the better
part of prejudice, constant exposure to ever more
facts ever more often repeated is the best hope of its
removal.

Conversion, in any case, is the wrong thing to look
for as the outcome of controversy. The reinforcement
of conviction or of loyalties by sound argument or
evidence is of itself a social gain, and this is achieved
in debate even when a listener only allows the echo
of his own point of view to register with him. More
than this often happens. However slowly, a modi-

[11] *Martin* v. *City of Struthers, Ohio,* 319, U.S. 141, 1943.
[12] *The People's Choice* by Paul Lazarsfeld. Duell, Sloan &
Pearce, 1945.

fied outlook and even reconciliation do take place, and the symbolic recognition that there are many sides to most questions, as affirmed in controversy on the air, is of itself a continuing social imperative.

But all this is in that will-o'-the-wisp realm of what follows after freedom from restraint. The purpose of this chapter is to plead for eternal vigilance regarding the specific and negative aspect of freedom — the desire to be rid of undesired restraints. It is a plea for the fresh declaration, where radio is concerned, of "eternal hostility against every form of tyranny over the mind of man."

V

Of Mice and Men

WITHOUT ADVERTISING, broadcasting, as we know it, would not exist. It is our radio's only source of revenue, accepted and acceptable in preference to any other known method of financing a very costly business. We cannot get something for nothing. A certain price has to be paid. The only question is how high a price makes for a fair exchange.

A great many programs that we hear, sponsored by advertisers, represent a fair balance of advantage. Some don't. There are flaws in the practice — and the blame for them cannot in fairness be laid entirely at the advertiser's door. The FCC, the Congress, and the public share the blame. In radio, as in our system of government, there is a division of powers. If power has become overconcentrated in one quarter, it is our fault as much as anybody's. With a full awareness, then, of our responsibility for what has happened, let us examine some of the flaws that have developed in a system that is basically sound.

Professor Harlow Shapley, famous scientist and lover of the arts, was listening to a symphony concert conducted by Arturo Toscanini. "The reception was fine, the mood was nothing short of ecstatic. . . . Our attentive listening had, in a sense, made us communicants in a majestic ethereal cathedral. We had collaborated in a timeless divine service. And then suddenly . . . a revolting, leering vulgarian defecated on the altar before us all, desecrating the cathedral . . . defaming the symphony and the artists. Before we could defend ourselves, a squalling, dissonant, hasty singing commercial burst in on the mood. . . . What we got was a hideous jingle about soap."

Thus, with a slick transition from symphony to soap, Professor Shapley was introduced to the radio advertiser's latest brain wave — the singing commercial. He was angry and he penned a letter, from which we have quoted, to the president of NBC. "I write this letter to you; but as I know that you probably cannot spare the time to hear personally from a listener, I am sending a copy of this letter to those distinguished citizens who are on the advisory committee of NBC."

But this was in 1944, and the advertiser has since thought of many a fresh trick by which to catch us unawares. New language has had to be invented to keep pace with his enterprising innovations. "Cow-catchers" and "hitchhikers" [1] are terms whose modern application Mr. Mencken will doubtless record in his monumental study of the American language. But he, like most of us, is a little behind the times. Like mice, we nibble at the bait before we are aware of the trap.

The traps are many and varied in design, and there is nowhere you can set them to greater advantage than in the house of Radio where mice abound. For the listener is the mousiest of mice and you have him where you want him. "If people like the show, the advertiser forces them to listen to his commercial; otherwise they don't get the show. Contrast this with newspaper or magazine, where a person may read articles or fiction without being forced to read the contiguous advertisement." [2] Take it away, boys. You're in the groove.

But that's not the half of it. You've forgotten the "spot" announcement. Ah, yes. The spot announcement; the neatest, cheapest, surest mousetrap on the

[1] A "cowcatcher" is a preceding plug for a minor product of the sponsor whose program is upcoming. A "hitchhiker" is a plug for another product of the sponsor of a program, following that for the product which the program is designed to advertise.

[2] *Brewer's Digest,* April 1945, p. 43.

market. "In the case of spot announcements the advertiser borrows an established audience, gets over his message quickly, before the listener gets up enough energy to turn it off." How's that for ingenuity? In and out, on borrowed time.

But even a mouse will turn, if the traps are set at every corner and the reek of cheese (or soap) is so strong as to spoil its appetite. Professor Shapley turned because a jingle broke in on a symphony. In 1945 a lot of smaller mice started turning over the "middle commercial" in newscasts. It all began with an editorial in the *St. Louis Post Dispatch* which, on January 18, called on the four major networks to quit interrupting newscasts with commercial plugs and to quit letting newscasts be sponsored by objectionable advertisers.

Other papers joined the hue and cry. A *Chicago Daily News* editorial lashed out against the "lush-voiced hams dramatizing trivial news items in one breath and extolling the virtues of El Stinko cigars in the next, without even changing his pace." The *Chicago Times* came across with this one: "There recently has developed a tendency toward shouting, screaming commercials that insult not only the intelligence but assault the ear in an unmerciful fashion." Advertisers rubbed their eyes. Since when, they asked themselves, were mousetraps instruments of mercy? Get into that trap, you mouse. "Otherwise you don't get the show."

Not to be outdone by the Middle West, the *New York Times* entered the fray, touching, incidentally, on a refinement of the middle commercial technique: —

The virtual subordination of radio's standards to the philosophy of advertising inevitably has led the networks into an unhealthy and untenable position. *It has permitted Gabriel Heatter to shift without emphasis from a discussion of the war to the merits of hair tonic.* It has forced the nation's best entertainers to act as candy butchers and debase their integrity as artists. It has permitted screeching voices to yell at our children to eat this or that if they want to be as efficient as some fictional character. . . . The broadcaster often has argued that it is not his function to "reform" the public taste, but, be that as it may, it certainly is the broadcaster's responsibility not to lower it.[3]

But it remained for a returning soldier to express a mood of which, with the return of eight million

[3] One radio commentator had had the courage to rebel long since, and won. "I made my own rebellion," says Raymond Swing, "on May 10, 1940, when writing my broadcast reporting German violation of French, Belgian, Dutch, and Luxembourg neutrality. It seemed hideous to have this account interrupted by a sales talk, and I balked."

men from war, we may hear more, for they have
viewed fresh horizons: —

> The aspect of home-front life which most dis-
> gusted me on return was radio. . . . The first eve-
> ning that I sat by a radio at home, I heard one long
> parade of headaches, coughs, aching muscles, stained
> teeth "unpleasant full feeling," and gastric hyper-
> acidity. . . . Our radio evenings are a sick parade
> of sicknesses and if they haven't yet made us a sick
> nation, I wonder why.

The radio industry, always sensitive to public opinion, was disturbed by these symptoms of endemic
indigestion. A few stations eliminated middle commercials from newscasts.

The Blue Network announced a new six-point policy modifying some of their more offensive characteristics but not banning middle commercials from
its news. NBC eliminated the middle commercial but
allowed a plug to fall anywhere within the first two
or the last three minutes of a fifteen-minute news-
cast, as a result of which the news period can now
be interrupted twice instead of once. CBS was plainly
irked by the whole affair. What was important, it
said, was not when the commercial was injected, but
how it was treated. Then, shifting its argument entirely, it protested that of its ten sponsored news
programs, only three carried middle commercials.

The National Association of Broadcasters (of which two networks and many independent stations are not members) later in the year produced new recommendations (which it is powerless to enforce) reducing the length of daytime plugs to the same amount of time (three minutes in a half-hour show) as already obtained for evening shows. *Broadcasting Magazine,* speaking for the industry, viewed the revolt of the public "with some trepidation." They felt, however, that much of the trouble was provoked by a relatively small group which "would put commercial radio in a strait jacket." Knowing both the public and the FCC they felt that "the current move will spend itself."

RAKE'S PROGRESS

As early as 1922 the dangers of excessive advertising had already been noted. In that year the first "Annual Radio Conference" was called by Mr. Herbert Hoover, then Secretary of Commerce. "It is inconceivable," he said, "that we should allow so great a possibility for service . . . to be drowned in advertising chatter."

No one, in those days, regarded such a view as eccentric or high hat. The conference itself, composed of representatives of the radio industry, was so much behind Mr. Hoover that it recommended that "direct advertising . . . be absolutely prohibited and that indirect advertising be limited to the announcements of the call letters of the station and the name of the concern responsible for the matter broadcasted." Radio, it seemed, was off to a promising start.

But as early as 1927 advertising abuses were among the first topics to engage the attention of the newly formed Federal Radio Commission, which came out with a sharp warning to the industry: "The amount and character of advertising must be rigidly confined within the limits consistent with the public service expected of the station." The Commission, moreover, meant what it said. A year later it refused to renew the license of Station WCRW in part because "it is clear that a large part of the program is distinctly commercial in character, consisting of advertisers' announcements and of direct advertising, including the quoting of prices."

But even with the passage of five years no gulf yet yawned between the views of government and industry on what constituted public interest. The spokesman of National Carbon Company, sponsors of the Ever-Ready Hour, thus explained the limits of what his company considered proper advertising to a House Committee in 1926: —

> . . . When these musical and semi-dramatic programs are given, we precede the program by some such announcement as this one, on December 15, 1925.

"Tuesday evening means the Ever-Ready Hour, for it is on this day and at this time each week that the National Carbon Company, makers of Ever-Ready flashlights and radio batteries, engages the facilities of these fourteen radio stations to present its artists in original radio creations. Tonight the sponsors of the hour have included in the program, and so forth."

Now, that is the extent of the advertising, direct or indirect, of any character which we do in connection with our program. . . . The statement of the name of your company or the sponsorship of the program must be delicately handled so that the listener will not feel that he is having advertising pushed over on him.

In 1929 the National Association of Broadcasters adopted "standards of commercial practice" which enjoined that "commercial announcements, as the term is generally understood, shall not be broadcast between 7 and 11 P.M."

How droll and old-fashioned that sounds to the sophisticated modern ear. One can see the smile of condescension on the face of our 1946 advertising executive. But those, after all, were horse-and-buggy days. Radio advertisers learned rapidly, and in another five years, by 1932, a real gulf yawned. That, indeed, was an awful year. The public had not yet learned its place. Its representatives in Congress were actively canvassing un-American ideas. The Senate passed a resolution that struck at the very root of our commercial system of broadcasting and brought consternation and terror to the advertiser. The Federal Radio Commission had been lax in the exercise of its powers as trustee for the people. The voice of Congress boomed out in official protest: —

Whereas there is growing dissatisfaction with the present use of radio facilities for purposes of commercial advertising: Be it "Resolved, That the Federal Radio Commission is hereby authorized and instructed to make a survey and to report to the Senate on the following questions:

1. What information there is available on the feasibility of Government ownership and operation of broadcasting facilities.

2. To what extent the facilities of a representative group of broadcasting stations are used for commercial advertising purposes.

3. To what extent the use of radio facilities for purposes of commercial advertising varies as between stations having power of one hundred watts, five hundred watts, one thousand watts, five thousand watts, and all in excess of five thousand watts.

4. What plans might be adopted to reduce, to limit, to control, and perhaps, to eliminate the use of radio facilities for commercial advertising purposes.

5. What rules or regulations have been adopted by other countries to control or to eliminate the use of radio facilities for commercial advertising purposes.

6. Whether it would be practicable and satisfactory to permit only the announcement of programs by persons or corporations."

The radio industry held its breath. To be or not to be, that was indeed the question. But the storm passed. The Commission, as we think, wisely recommended no basic change in our commercial system. Regulation and self-regulation, it felt, would eliminate abuses. The ascendancy of the commercial broadcaster was never again so rudely challenged. Year by year and bit by bit standards of public interest and convenience have slipped, advertising has crept in, and the gulf between public and commercial interest has widened. Let us dismiss the twenties as radio's "amateur hour" and move on into the thirties.

In 1930 a station owner and then president of the National Association of Broadcasters, giving evidence before a Senate committee, was able to claim that "in our station no more than one minute out of every thirty minutes is devoted to advertising sponsorship." Asked by the chairman, "Do all the advertisers on your station confine themselves to that?" he answered,

"Some of them do not use as much as that." At the same hearings the president of CBS was able to boast that on his network "seven tenths of 1 per cent of all our time" alone is given to commercial advertising.[4]

But as the thirties advanced, standards relaxed progressively. From 1937 to mid-1945 the code of the National Association of Broadcasters has allowed the following amount of time for advertising (with some convenient exceptions that allow for more on certain types of programs): —

Daytime

2 minutes in a 5-minute program
3¼ minutes in a 15-minute program
4½ minutes in a 30-minute program

Nighttime

1¾ minutes in a 5-minute program
2½ minutes in a 15-minute program
3 minutes in a 30-minute program

Thus a clever advertiser, bent on securing the maximum of time for advertising, could defeat even these generous provisions by buying six consecutive five-minute program periods in the daytime and putting on twelve minutes of advertising in half an hour!

[4] Senate Committee on Interstate Commerce Hearings on S. 6. 71st Congress, 2nd Session.

Nor is the NAB code universally observed, either by its members or, naturally, by the hundreds of non-member stations. The writer has, for example, listened to one commercial plug which ran five consecutive minutes without program "interruption."

On "spot" announcements which are superimposed on the sponsor's legitimate plug in the program period for which he has paid, *no limit whatsoever has ever been set* by the NAB. An extreme example of the license which advertisers are ready to indulge is that of a station which, in January 1945, broadcast 2215 commercial spot announcements in 135 hours. This is an average of 16.7 "spots" an hour throughout an entire week.

We have, indeed, now reached such a pass that some of the more enlightened stations are cashing in on a restraint which, in a sane society, would be taken for granted. They are conceding us as a privilege what should be a right. "We now bring you the news," they say, *"uninterrupted"!* And since beggars cannot be choosers, we sit back with a "thank you" on our lips.

THE ANATOMY OF MELANCHOLY

Our methods of dealing with criminals are crude. We put them behind bars. This is unimaginative and

not always effective. We should do better if we made
the punishment fit the crime. For the "criminals" of
the advertising fraternity we want to suggest a punishment that fits. We propose that they replace, until
cured, the forgotten men in this melancholy business
— officials in the Federal Trade Commission who, in
the public interest, scrutinize advertising copy for
infringement of the Pure Food and Drug Act.

Consider these men's lives. In 1944 the Federal
Trade Commission examined 627,719 commercial radio broadcast continuities. "The continuities examined totaled 1,523,000 typewritten pages. . . . An
average of 4866 pages of radio script was read each
working day. From this material 19,512 advertising
broadcasts were marked for further study as containing representations that might be false or misleading."[5]

A large amount of the material examined by these
unsung defenders of the public interest deals with
health cures. Most of it gets by, for advertisers have
become adept in observing the letter of the law.
Phrases are used that skate deftly over the thin ice
of truth. There is no lie — in words — but a wealth of
deceptive innuendo. Radio communication has this
advantage over print — to the innuendo of the phrase
it adds opportunity for innuendo of the voice. "By a

[5] Annual Report of the Federal Trade Commission.

clever use of inflection the announcer for one headache tablet uses the very words, which warn of possible danger, to minimize the danger and promote
the product. 'Of course,' he says, in a condescending,
almost scornful pianissimo, 'if your headaches persist
you should see your doctor. But . . . [crescendo]
. . . for prompt, welcome relief from nagging
pain . . .' and so on. If you're sensible, the implication is, you'll buy those tablets." [6]

The radio listener is never advised to consult a
doctor first. First, buy the patent cure. Then, if it
fails, run to your doctor. The radio advertiser concentrates on symptoms. He addresses millions without knowledge of the condition of any one of them.
Headaches and constipation and the rest of the
pleasant subjects that we hear about are almost
invariably occasioned by some deeper-seated disorder. To treat the symptom may relieve a pain, remove discomfort. It is unlikely to remove the disorder, for the "cure" doesn't deal with the disorder.
It may even aggravate it. Danger for somebody is
latent in most of the health cures offered on the radio.

The Federal Trade Commission, poring over its
4866 pages a day, may pick up, in time, violations of

[6] R. M. Cunningham in the *New Republic*, October 23,
1944.

the letter of the law.[7] Many an advertiser, probably doing untold damage to untold ignorant, suggestible listeners, will get away with it. Radio and the advertiser take the cash. The public takes the kicks.

Networks and stations alike carry these modern counterparts of the one-time peddler of patent medicines. A few have troubled consciences. But the course of virtue is not made easy for them. One of radio's most enlightened and responsible operators is Mr. Nathan Straus, president of Station WMCA in New York. This is the story that he told in the columns of the *New York Times*, June 3, 1945: —

> Something else that disturbs us in particular concerns the advertising of patent medicines. This is a touchy subject because the manufacturers of patent medicines spend hundreds of millions of dollars in advertising their products. The fact that the therapeutic value of many of the products advertised is dubious and that some are potentially dangerous, as physicians privately admit, cannot be viewed with indifference.

[7] But even they are handicapped. Before a House Labor Committee their assistant chief counsel said the FTC didn't have the funds to police even medicine advertising properly. He said a lot of work was being done, however. The committee chairman rather cruelly rejoined, "You don't seem to be making any headway from the noise we hear over the air." (Reported in *Variety*, May 23, 1945.)

As an example of the radio operator's problem, we recently turned down a program advertising a notorious patent medicine which has been exposed as worthless. The account, representing $25,000 a year, went to another station. We had incurred the ill-will of an advertiser and an advertising agency — without accomplishing anything that would tend to raise the standards of patent medicine advertising.

Our unsuccessful efforts to improve such a condition are worth recounting. First, we approached the New York Academy of Medicine. We asked to submit for their approval all medical and patent medicine advertising offered to us. In turn, should the Academy disapprove a product, we asked permission to state the fact to the advertiser and the advertising agency as justification for our refusal to accept it. After several long discussions, the Academy officials said that they could give us general advice but that they could not assume the kind of responsibility implicit in the agreement which we proposed.

We then appealed to the United States Public Health Service. They told us that, because of their diversified responsibilities, they could not participate in such a project.

Our experience points, I think, to the need for a plan that will assure listeners that any statement made on the air about a medical product may be accepted without reservation. This would seem to require the participation of an outside institution of admitted competence and unquestionable integrity.

A touchy subject, involving hundreds of millions of dollars, lucrative accounts — and the health and self-respect of a nation.

But not only are ignorance, credulity, sickness of mind and body played on and the law side-stepped. Not even our deepest emotions are inviolate, for the "artful dodger" has side-stepped yet another law. Public Law 623, approved on June 22, 1942, provides that "the flag should never be used for advertising purposes *in any manner whatsoever.*" The flag, symbol of patriotism and of loyalties that for nearly four agonizing years were foremost in the minds and hearts of all Americans. But never mind symbolism. Stick to the letter of the law. It says "the flag." That gives us an out. You can't wave a flag at a microphone. Television isn't here yet. So let's get going. "Association of ideas." That's in every textbook of psychology. Let's work that one.

A voice at the microphone is speaking. Listen, America.

"As every one of you well knows, the United States is face to face with a great challenge. People everywhere are seriously concerned about the nation's all-out effort. Regardless of how or where you serve, your first duty is . . ." What's coming? Is it a message from the President, some new war measure, call to sacrifice? No, this is radio. It's a call to duty for BC Headache Powder. The voice goes on, pitched up a little higher. "Your first duty is to keep well. . . . When a simple headache develops, or the pain of neuralgia strikes, try a BC Headache Powder. The quick-acting prescription-type ingredients in the BC formula usually work fast and relieve in a hurry. Remember this. Get one of the 25-cent packages of BC TODAY . . . and *consult a physician when pains persist or recur frequently.*"

But you've tried BC? And it doesn't work? Why, that's all right. Try *Anacin.* Listen, mister, "with 75,000 doctors and nurses in the armed forces, it's more necessary than ever to guard your health. . . . Why suffer from the pains of simple headache or minor neuralgia when Anacin gives such incredibly fast, effective relief?"

War and health. But how about war and hair?

1st Voice. You know, friends, right now millions of servicemen are getting training that will make them far better civilians. They're learning new peacetime trades . . .

2nd Voice (*filter*). Welding . . . auto repair . . . radio operation . . . electric refrigeration . . .

1st Voice (*interrupting*). What's more, our men in uniform are given a priceless opportunity for better educations . . .

2ND VOICE (*filter*). Free courses in . . . mathematics . . . foreign languages . . . biology . . . English literature . . .

1ST VOICE (*interrupting*). Our servicemen also learn valuable lessons in personal appearance . . .

2ND VOICE (*filter*). Teeth brushed . . . clothes clean . . . hair neat . . . shoes shined . . .

1ST VOICE (*interrupting*). Yes, as part of their training for service our men learn many valuable lessons in good grooming. Thousands, for example, discover how Vitalis . . . the famous hair-grooming preparation . . . can give their appearance a real boost.

Who can do anything about it? The Federal Trade Commission is understaffed, and anyhow is only concerned with the strict observance of the law. The Federal Communications Commission is debarred from censorship. Its predecessor, the Federal Radio Commission, did define general principles and, on occasion, acted on them. The FCC has for eleven years been largely silent and inactive. Its present chairman has written and spoken about advertising and other current abuses in radio, and has implicitly served notice on the industry that the Commission may take some action unless a housecleaning takes place.

But a good case can be made against Commission action on this specific subject. Beyond a ruling, surely feasible, against the use of advertising for the propagation of ideas, as contrasted with goods, no regulation, any more than any law, can stop up all the loopholes. Commission action *may* be forced — either by public pressure or by the Congress — to limit, for example, the length and frequency of advertising matter.

But such action would seem unfortunate. It would be assailed as arbitrary by the trade, it would be difficult to enforce and, however carefully phrased, it might work hardships on some. And it would and could only curb some of the abuses. There is no rule that can regulate taste, control innuendo, or prevent the exploitation of human emotions. Advertisers rendered a real service, during the war years, by lending their audiences to government messages and appeals for action. By no means all, or even a majority, "used" patriotism as a tag for selling goods.

The public can do something. But it is slow to rouse. Extremities are reached before public reaction sets in. Hence the wild swinging of the pendulum to which the current operation of radio is subject. And public agitation is hard to sustain. *Broadcasting Magazine* was right in anticipating that "the current mood will spend itself." Even responsible associations, as Mr. Straus sadly discovered, are too cautious to commit themselves. Timidity and lethargy afflict us. Nearly everyone is scared of vested interests and too few people have a sense of righteous indignation. We drift, we accept, we grow, even, to like what we get.

Many listeners must have applauded, but few would themselves voice publicly the sentiment of one courageous and candid writer during the flare-up of 1945: —

> I am sick of this disgusting practice, sick of the men who read the brave or tragic developments of the day sandwiched in between oily pleas for some commodity. . . . Is there no God but sales and profits? Is there no bottom to the depth to which human greed and merchandising can sink? . . . Are there any of us free enough of the love of a dollar to cry "stop it" and see that it is stopped? [8]

Alas, all too few. Have we the right, then, to expect of those whose business is merchandising that they should "stop it" of their own accord? No one who has not in some way registered his protest can answer that with either confidence or a good conscience. And yet the only answer is affirmative. On every ground — of public interest, of ultimate self-

[8] Paul Gallico in May 1945 *Esquire*.

interest, of common decency — self-regulation is the desirable and the only sure solution. No one in his senses needs to quarrel with the system of radio that we have. Advertising is its source of revenue. And, as Professor Shapley put it in his letter, "The vast audience would have been quite willing at that time to hear General Motors tell of further concert plans or even tell, with dignity suitable to the occasion, about the products of General Motors." But then, as he also put it, "A high official in the broadcasting industry recently defended such tricks: and he said to me in effect, 'Are we to be guided by what a few of you intellectuals think? Our surveys show that the people want these singing commercials.'"

Fortunately not all advertisers and radio executives subscribe to such a view. There are still pioneers in radio. But Professor Shapley's "high official" seems to dominate the scene, prescribe too much of the medicine. There are two schools of thought contending for ascendancy.

VI

A Matter of Money

IN AN OPEN letter to the Federal Communications Commission on August 7, 1945, Congressman Celler charged it with failure to protect the public interest in its administration, and indicted the radio industry for "ignoring its responsibilities to the public in favor of money making operations." In previous chapters we have noted some of the effects on program service of radio's dollar philosophy. But there are certain aspects of this matter of money that remain to be considered. Let us consider three questions: Where does the money come from which makes radio possible? What influence on radio may the man with the money have? What is the public's interest and the FCC's responsibility regarding the monetary aspect of radio's administration?

Who Pays for Radio?

In seeking the good will and support of the public, big business has attempted to propagate a convenient but misleading idea. Its public-relations experts have sought to persuade us that it is to big business, in terms of its annual investment of millions of dollars in radio, that we owe the fine program services we get. Accompanying this questionable claim there is often the suggestion that we, the public, are therefore somehow beholden to the advertiser and to the networks and stations, as though a benefit had been conferred for which we should be grateful. There is no doubt that many innocent listeners genuinely feel beholden in this way and regard themselves as fortunate beneficiaries of a generous patron. This is a dangerously sentimental state of mind, implying a subservience on the part of the public which is neither justified nor healthy. Business is not philanthropy. It is a system of exchange. The businessman provides us with the goods and we provide him with his profits. We can cry quits on the deal. We should never feel subservient or anything but incidentally grateful.

But the idea that big business alone (in the guise of radio's sponsors and the stations that bring radio into our houses) provides the wherewithal for programs is itself a fallacy. If gratitude enters in at all it is owed by the radio industry and by big business to the listener. The thanks, at the moment, are on the wrong lips. Consider the facts.

The outlay, in capital and running costs, of advertisers and the radio industry is admittedly considerable. *But so is ours.* As of December 31, 1943, the tangible property of networks and stations amounted to an original cost of $81,148,128. Our property, as represented by the purchase of receiving sets, amounted to an original cost of about $2,078,000,000.[1] In other words, *we, the public, have invested in radio a sum that exceeds that of the industry's investment by twenty-six to one.* If you prefer to consider depreciated values — the industry's and ours — the depreciated value of our property exceeds that of the industry's by a margin of about seventeen to one.

Or consider the advertiser, who also claims to foot the bill. In 1944 the advertiser's total expenditure, in what was a record year, amounted to some $396,946,991. That is a lot of money. But what did *we* spend, over and above our original outlay on sets? According to *Radio and Television Retailing* (January 1945) the listener's expenditure on electricity, batteries, replacements, and repairs and depreciation charges on receiving sets totaled some $632,000,000. Thus, assuming 55 million receiving sets in use, our expenditure each day amounted to about 3.1 cents, while the advertiser spent about 2.0 cents. This, of

[1] *Radio & Television Retailing,* Jan. 1945, p. 21.

course, quite apart from our contributions to the advertiser by responding, with purchase of his wares, to his sales talk on the air. In the light of these figures the listener is, perhaps, entitled to raise his head and claim his rights a little less diffidently than heretofore.

When it comes to profits, we have a more difficult equation to work out. Our profit is intangible, consisting of satisfaction with what we hear and a full measure of public service to all the different interests comprised by the listening public. The profits of the radio industry can be reckoned in hard cash. In 1944, networks and commercial stations earned a net income, subject to tax, of approximately $90,000,000. This amounts to a return on the original cost of their tangible property of 108.8 per cent a year. Or, if you take account of the depreciated value of this property, *their return amounts to 222.6 per cent a year*. This is nice going — for the industry. It looks as if there were some room for curtailment of profit in the public interest which would still leave the radio industry some distance off from bankruptcy.

THE MAN WITH THE POCKETBOOK

"He who controls the pocketbook controls the man," said the president of a great network, inviting our interest in the personal equation of radio's management as it affects our radio services. Different men make different use of their pocketbooks. The following story of a station that shall be nameless shows how vital an interest each of us has in this matter of the man and his control of his pocketbook.

Station X enjoys the privilege of using one of the best broadcasting channels in the country, with 50,000 watts of power. It began operations in 1925 when the station was dedicated to the city and the state "and to the service of their people in such ways as may be found most useful to them." Its standards were high, even purist at the start. Station X "has endeavored to be a distinctive personality among broadcasting stations. To attain this end its programs have maintained high musical and artistic standards. The station's No Jazz policy is indicative." At one time over 90 per cent of its programs were rendered by its own studio organizations. At one time, too, the station had ten orchestras or chamber-music combinations and even ran its own opera company.

But in 1935 the station changed hands. It was bought by a holding company. An absentee landlord is not necessarily a bad one, but he can hardly be expected to maintain the same pride and interest as a landlord on the spot. At any rate, the transfer of Station X coincided with some interesting changes in the tone and character of its program services. He who now controlled the pocketbook had different ideas about how its contents should be disbursed.

By 1944 the station had become a real business concern. For a week in 1944, 87.5 per cent of its time, between eight in the morning and eleven o'clock at night, was monopolized by commercial programs. On every day of the week, except Saturday and Sunday, commercial programs occupied fourteen out of fifteen hours. During the best listening hours, between 6 and 11 P.M., 96.9 per cent of the time was commercial. Monday through Friday, there was not one sustaining program between 2 P.M. and 11 P.M. During the week nine hours and fifty minutes of religious programs were broadcast: all but thirty minutes were paid for at commercial rates. Nearly two thirds of the religion broadcast was "canned" — that is, mass produced and shipped into the community on transcribed platters. The city served by Station X has more than 450 churches of its own.

In 1943 the station had a gross income of about a million dollars. After covering all expenses, $610,000 was left as clear profit before federal income tax, while out of each dollar of revenue the station spent three cents on program talent. Its profit represented a return of 265 per cent on the depreciated value of its entire investment in broadcasting property.

This real life story raises some interesting questions. A property that enables a man to earn 265 per cent on its depreciated value is tempting bait. It seems tempting, also, to inquire whether the public has not some interest in the relation between profits made and service rendered.

The listener of course has no right to concern himself with a station owner's profits — *except as these reflect adversely on program service rendered.* Fair exchange is no robbery, but in radio, even more than in ordinary business, the fairness of exchange is paramount, not only because of the nature of the commodity purveyed — ideas and information and entertainment — but because the broadcaster is lessee of a public property. By the standards we have set in this book, the bare facts and figures quoted above on the program performance of this station are sufficient, without fuller scrutiny, to warrant a complaint. More cash is being taken out of the till than is being put in by way of program service. Profits and performance are inextricably interlinked.

This would seem to lead to the conclusion that, in the public domain of broadcasting, we the people have a right to a good deal of information (which in ordinary business could fairly be claimed to be private) regarding the earnings, the financial setup and contractual arrangements of networks and stations.

For all these bear directly on the program service rendered in a public domain. Such information is made available to the Federal Communications Commission. But in a recent decision (August 3, 1945) the Commission closed its doors on this matter to the public. We are not to be allowed to know the facts. One lone, dissenting vote was cast. As many people, concerned about the road that radio is taking, are likely to rally to his point of view, the dissenting opinion of Commissioner C. J. Durr deserves quotation in part: —

> Is [radio] essentially private business tinged only with such public interest as may flow as an incidental byproduct of profit-making operations, or is it essentially public business? . . . The commission itself recognizes the public nature of broadcasting by requiring the information in question to be filed with it. . . . No cloak of secrecy should keep from the public the information upon which the commission relies, whether in deciding individual cases or in determining matters of broad policy. . . .
>
> Broadcasters are strongly insistent upon a maximum of regulation by the public and a minimum of regulation by the Government. They should not at the same time seek to conceal from the public the information essential to intelligent public regulation.

Another aspect of this matter of money is the question of the price involved in the transfer of station ownership; and not only the price but the character and qualifications of the purchaser who is now to control the purse.

During the war, with all construction permits canceled, purchase of a radio station has been the only means of breaking into radio's magic circle. The property has therefore acquired a high scarcity value, and some stations, since 1939, have been changing hands at fantastic figures. Many have realized from four to ten times the value of all their assets. In one instance the sale price was more than thirty times the original cost. In another, a station sold for 1534 times its net income!

Evidently it is not the property alone that counts but the opportunity, afforded by possession of the property, to acquire also the frequency that goes with it. The FCC itself recognizes the danger. "It seems clear that in transfer cases, particularly in recent years, the transferees in paying sums in excess of the value of the physical properties and good will *are making payments for the expectancy that an existing license will be renewed.*" [2]

The dangers are obvious. An exorbitant price paid for a station, out of all proportion to the value of the property acquired, may mean, in plain language, a trafficking in *licenses*. Again, it may well involve the

[2] In the matter of Powel Crosley, Jr., Transferor, and the Aviation Corporation, Transferee Docket No. 6767.

purchaser in the overcommercialization of his program services. He is likely to be forced to sell time
(as does Station X) at the expense of public interest in order to secure a return on his huge capital
investment. It means, too, that when a station is
transferred, it goes to the highest bidder. Is the public interest best served when the operation of a station passes, automatically, to the man with the most
cash in his pocketbook?

The price a man pays for acquiring a radio station
is a price paid for the key to a public domain. His
capacity to operate in the public interest is affected
by the price he pays, for he must recover a reasonable return on his investment. Again, his interest in
rendering a public service, as contrasted with an exclusive or predominant interest in making profits,
likewise affects the character of programs he is likely
to put out.

And what of the man's character, outlook, and
chief preoccupations? His previous interest in radio
as a public service, his awareness of its social and
political significance, are, surely, relevant considerations when he applies for the right of access to this
public domain. Is his radio station his main interest
or is it merely a subordinate and incidental interest,
just one of a package of properties that he is acquiring as part of the over-all investment of his capital?

Is the public not concerned? Such questions lend peculiar interest to a decision made by the public's guardian, the Federal Communications Commission, in September 1945. Here is the story.

Powel Crosley, Jr., Prepares to Die

Mr. Powel Crosley is a rich man. The book value of all his properties amounts to about thirteen million dollars. He began as a manufacturer of automobile parts and of various household appliances. He was an early pioneer in radio and became one of the great barons of this vast empire. He has a license to operate or experiment with twenty-three radio stations in the AM, FM, television fields. These include five short-wave international transmitters and four international telegraph stations.

But he is also the possessor of a very juicy plum — Station WLW in Cincinnati. This is one of the most powerful stations in the country. Its primary coverage, both day and night, extends over 72,000 square miles, blanketing a population of about six and one half millions. Its area of secondary nighttime coverage extends over twenty-five of the forty-eight states.

Mr. Crosley has been concerned with radio for twenty-three years. But Mr. Crosley is fifty-nine years old and he is mindful of death. He is concerned about the future welfare of his properties. He wants to sell out. In testifying before the FCC, he said that his principal reason for wanting to sell his properties was a desire to have his corporation "in strong hands" in the event of his death. Strong hands had been extended to him, to relieve him of his burden of anxiety, by the Aviation Corporation, and he wanted to sell all his properties to them.

The activities of the Aviation Corporation and of those who control its interests range from the manufacture of kitchen sinks and steel cabinets to the conduct of a brokerage business and include the manufacture of airplanes, ships, steel, and the control of a large public-utility holding company. They also have substantial interests in American Airlines, Inc., and Pan-American Airways, Inc. Their hands are not only strong but have a very wide grasp.

The deal for transfer of Mr. Crosley's properties was almost completed when AVCO struck a snag. At the start of the negotiations, AVCO *had no intention or desire to acquire the Crosley broadcasting stations,* even though it "knew that Crosley was the owner of Station WLW." But when Mr. Crosley explained that "for tax reasons" he was reluctant to segregate them, AVCO agreed to buy the "entire package."

It was at this point that AVCO was tactfully advised of the existence of the Federal Communications Commission and of certain regulatory requirements, under the law, attendant on the transfer of a station owner's license. But the advice came uncomfortably late. The proposed contract for purchase of the Crosley Corporation was originally due to expire on July 16, 1945, but the application to the FCC, for their consent, was only filed on June 2 and the case was designated for hearing on July 10. So the date of expiration of the contract was deferred to August 16, the parties descended on Washington, urged the Commission to advance the date of its hearings, and threatened that "a delay in the hearing would place the Crosley Corporation in an extremely disadvantageous competitive position." The Commission had important and urgent business on its hands (including the whole question of new regulations for FM broadcasting) but agreed to advance the date of its hearings. After these hearings the proposed transfer was approved, but by a split vote of four to three, and only after the disclosure of some very revealing facts. The following were only some of the tastier morsels.

Previous experience of broadcasting cannot, obviously, be demanded of a person on first entering the field. But one might expect that an applicant would have made himself reasonably familiar with the law, as it relates to broadcasting, the statutory regulations made by the FCC, and the general question of what constitutes the public interest as far as programs are concerned. In this case we must make generous allowance for the applicant for, as we have seen, AVCO had originally "no intention or desire" to acquire Mr. Crosley's interests in broadcasting. Their general knowledge test must be simple and minimal in its demands. But radio has a certain social importance. In the interest of public safety even an automobile driver's license is not granted on a "commitment" to become acquainted — at some later date — with the traffic laws. AVCO, under cross-examination, proved long on commitments but a little short on knowledge. Let us sit in on the hearings.

The law forbids the granting of a radio license to any corporation in which more than 25 per cent of stock is owned by aliens. AVCO had no idea what percentage of its stockholders were aliens but it quickly issued a "postcard inquiry" to find out.

As we have seen, the price for which a station changes hands has an important bearing on its operations. What was the proposed price for the Crosley broadcasting properties? No figure could be given. The stock transfer was based on the purchase

of all the assets as "a package of equities." Station
WLW and the twenty-three domestic and international licenses that went with it were just part of the
bundle. There "was no necessity of placing any
value" on any or all of them.

Station WLW is situated in Cincinnati. Did the
directors of AVCO reside there? No. Had they acquainted themselves with listeners' needs in the
area covered by the station and with talent available?
No. Were they familiar with the present programs
and did they approve of them? They were not familiar, but a "personal and independent investigation will be made to determine whether Station
WLW is fulfilling its statutory duties."

The chief witnesses for AVCO were Mr. Victor
Emanuel and Mr. Irving B. Babcock, the corporation's chief executive and the second-in-command.
"Mr. Emanuel," and we quote from the statement of
the dissenting commissioners, "had 'never considered
the question' as to how much time the board of
directors of AVCO would spend on the broadcasting
activities." He "had 'never even considered the question' as to whether there was any intention to increase the profits from broadcasting operations. . . .
He knew 'admittedly very little about broadcasting.'
. . . He knew 'nothing at all' about international
broadcasting in which his company is acquiring a

dominant position. . . . He had not read the Communications Act or attempted to inform himself in any way as to the responsibilities of a broadcasting license. The application filed with the Commission . . . stated that 'approval of this application will provide for the betterment of services now provided.' When asked what definite plans the transferee had for the betterment of the service, he stated that 'we have no definite plans.'. . . In answer to a question as to what, in his opinion, constituted a good program balance, the best reply he could give was 'My conception would be the kind of a job that would best serve every man, woman and child in America.'"

Asked about the cost of the construction of FM and television stations, for which applications had been filed with the Commission, Mr. Emanuel thought it was about $250,000 for FM but was "not surprised" when told that the actual estimate was $2,135,000, or nearly ten times the amount that he had mentioned.

Mr. Babcock was likewise ignorant of the law and the regulations. On WLW's present programs he had not "enough information to recommend any change." He thought that the best time for sustaining programs would be "late at night . . . around midnight." Later he qualified this remarkable opinion by one equally remarkable, claiming that a station could render a satisfactory service if 100 per cent of its time was commercially sponsored.

But time was pressing. Any delay in approving the transfer would be "extremely disadvantageous" to the parties' competitive position. The commissioners deliberated, and the majority, waiving such evidence as the above, gave AVCO the benefit of such doubts as may have assailed them. AVCO, originally without "intention or desire" to acquire an interest in radio, had by the time of the hearings discovered an extraordinary enthusiasm for it. The directors, according to Mr. Emanuel, "have become tremendously interested and enthused," and even Mr. Babcock admitted that he had become "quite interested." This was reassuring.

That doubts did in fact assail those who signed their names to the decision is evident from a supplement to their statement. They decided to hold public hearings on a proposed new procedure. Under this plan, the Commission and the seller would publish the terms of a proposed station sale and other persons than the prospective buyer would be invited to put up their bid. "The Commission would consider *all* applications on their merits, with a *view to granting the transfer on the basis of public interest.*" Could it be that in this AVCO case, to which this new plan was appended as an afterthought, transfer was not granted in the public interest?

But AVCO raised more problems than that of the preselection by a station of a successor to the throne. What are proper qualifications for a station licensee? To what extent should "holding companies, investment banking groups, large industrial empires, large manufacturing companies," be allowed to control radio stations? What yardstick should be used "for measuring the appropriate value of a station" to preclude sales at artificial prices? Exhausted by their labors over AVCO the Commission decided to refer these matters for decision to the Congress.[3]

These afterthoughts are a welcome sign that the Commission is awaking at long last from its intermittent slumber and facing (if not tackling) some of the fundamental democratic issues raised by radio. Regrettable and puzzling is the fact that so momentous a decision as that involved "in the matter of Powel Crosley, Jr., and Aviation Corporation" should have been taken, rather than deferred, while the commissioners were still sleepwalking in a trance of indecision and perplexity. The grounds for the majority decision in the AVCO case are worth brief summary.

1. *Technical requirements of the law.* The major-

---

[3] But six months later Congress had not yet been approached on these matters.

ity found that AVCO met the citizenship requirements of the Communications Act and was finan-
cially and technically qualified.

2. *Purchase price.* While no price could be named
for purchase of the radio property, they could find
"no evidence of trafficking in licenses and the record
showed that the price paid would not adversely affect
AVCO's responsibility or the station's program structure." To deny the application, "the Commission
would reverse 17 years of precedent and establish
new policies." They were forced to admit that a "re-
tiring broadcaster is very apt to be more influenced
by the size of his prospective purchaser's pocketbook
than by the type of service which the purchaser plans
to offer to the public," but felt helpless to do anything about it. The Communications Act didn't tell
them exactly what to do. And, as they reviewed past
precedent, they found that "more than half of existing licenses were not selected by the Commission on
the basis of competitive application but . . . by some
transferor." They judged that this was no time to
make a change and, in view of the powerful interests
involved, it is not difficult to guess why.

3. *Big-business control of radio.* They were evidently aware of the dangers of big business taking
over broadcasting as a "mere adjunct of the principal
business," but they thought the applicants had shown

themselves aware of their responsibility and were happy to accept their "*commitment* [*sic*] to become fully acquainted with the Communications Act and the applicable regulations [and] to study [*sic*] the present program structure of Station WLW." On the "complete ignorance" of witnesses about international broadcasting, they were discreetly silent. Because a great many present licensees have a principal business interest in some other enterprise than broadcasting, the majority of the commissioners considered themselves bound by past precedent. To reverse this questionable precedent would "throw the broadcast industry into a state of chaos."

Now let us summarize the opinion of the dissenting commissioners.

1. *Information vital to decision.* The Communications Act provides that no license shall be transferred, "unless the Commission shall, after securing full information, decide that said transfer is in the public interest." [4] AVCO's failure to provide any information whatsoever on the vital question of the purchase price of the radio properties deprived the Commission of its opportunity to comply with a specific and positive

[4] It is significant that one of the few changes in the law made by the Congress, when enacting the Communications Act, was the inclusion of this specific demand for "full information" before approval of a station's transfer.

requirement of the law. The minority felt, moreover, that they could not rest content with mere "assurances . . . that the over-all consideration will not have an adverse effect on the station's program structure. . . . Our unwillingness is increased by the testimony of the president of AVCO that he believed it possible for a station to operate in the public interest even though 100 per cent of its time should be sold to commercial sponsors."

2. *The significance of precedent.* "No licensee," say the minority, "has any vested interest in the Commission's past mistakes or omissions. . . . If this Commission were bound to inaction by the failure of its predecessors to act, no substantive improvement in regulatory techniques could ever be introduced." The majority, it is further argued, "concludes that the Commission has no authority to disapprove the present transfer, 'unless past precedents are ignored.' Here, admittedly, regulatory responsibility, imposed by Congress, is being abdicated in favor of precedents, in order to confer a security of tenure upon licensees at the sacrifice of public interest." In any case the precedents cited are of an ex parte nature. In 1932, for instance, the Federal Radio Commission agreed unanimously that applications for a license should be accompanied by a sworn statement show-

ing not merely the price to be paid but an itemized statement of the individual cost of each item transferred.

3. *Big-business control of radio.* AVCO is a holding company.

On this matter the minority commented as follows: "This is a type of corporate structure which has long been a matter of concern to the people of this country and to Congress itself because of its effectiveness as a device by which small groups of individuals, through the use of other people's money, are enabled to dominate large segments of our national economy without any corresponding responsibility to the public which is so vitally affected by their operations, or even to their stockholders whose proxies they use to solidify their positions of power. If to this concentration of economic power there is added the tremendous power of influencing public opinion which goes with the operation of major broadcasting facilities, domestic and international, the result is the creation of a repository of power able to challenge the sovereignty of government itself. Efforts on the part of corporate holding companies to control newspapers have traditionally met with widespread public concern and disapproval. Certainly there is full justification for an equal, if not greater, public concern and disapproval over the acquisition of broadcasting facilities by similar business aggregations. We do not believe that the 'larger and more effective use of radio in the public interest' will be encouraged by giving such transfers the stamp of official approval."

4. *Purchase price.* The Commission expressly asked, ahead of time, for information about the price to be paid for WLW and the international broadcast stations and, in so doing, recognized this as a proper matter of inquiry. It was refused such information. How, then, could it judge whether trafficking in licenses was going on? "We cannot agree," say the minority, "that the Commission must limit its concern to the problem of trafficking in licenses only [to] where it can be shown that the licensee acquired his license with the original intention of reselling it at a profit. No licensee should be permitted to profit by the sale of publicly owned frequencies, whether his intention to sell was acquired before or after he became the licensee. We recognize that there is no mathematical formula pursuant to which the Commission can investigate the sale price of a station. . . . This requires an exercise of judgment applied to the circumstances in each case. The difficulty of the problem in no way absolves the Commission from re-

sponsibility. If it were possible for Congress to lay down exact rules applicable to all the problems of broadcasting . . . there would be no need for a Commission." As to speculation, of which the majority found no evidence, "it is difficult to see how any evidence, one way or the other, could be contained in a record which does not even disclose the price at which the broadcasting facilities are being transferred."

5. *Knowledge of programing.* "Programing is the essence of broadcasting and yet not a single witness for the transferee demonstrated more than the vaguest idea about the kind of program service which would be rendered, the availability of program talent and sources, the needs of the people in WLW's service area, or even about the type of program service being rendered under the previous management."

Thus the majority and the dissenting minority in a transfer case which is perhaps the most important that ever came before the Commission.

The sincerity of those who put their name to this decision is not in question. What we may fairly question is their discretion, their courage, and the service they have rendered to the public interest. The case is puzzling and disturbing on several counts.

As Commissioner Ray Wakefield put it, "the record indicates nothing imminent which requires the

Powel Crosley family to dispose of their present radio holdings. Ample time is apparently available for it to find a transferee who is a worthy successor, who has an interest in broadcasting as such and who does not consider the purchase of radio properties as 'a package of equities.'" An immediate issue was forced only by Mr. Crosley's insistence on selling all his properties at once, thereby limiting the field of possible purchasers to such as could lay their hands on more than twenty million dollars. Has a private citizen the right thus to limit access to a public domain?

Indeed, the whole transaction appears to have involved unseemly haste, a much too eager deference to the convenience of private interests, a less than responsible concern for public and, indeed, national interests. The whim of an individual was allowed to create and, in effect, to decide the issue. Approval was pushed through within seven weeks from the date it was announced, while many other, less important transfers have hung fire for many months. Even more remarkable, the decision was announced some weeks before the Commission's opinion was issued, suggesting that the Commission voted first and deliberated afterwards.

Moreover the logic of the majority commissioners' decision does not hang together. They admit on the one hand that the case "presents grave questions *of*

public policy." But in the same breath they admit,
implicitly, that they have neither a clear view as to
how such questions of public policy should be decided nor any confidence that they are legally empowered thus to interpret policy. The AVCO case,
they say, illustrates a problem which they are con-
strained to put up to the Congress for a ruling. *Yet
they themselves rule on the case.*

"When, as in the instant case, the public interest
will not be adversely affected [*sic*] by adhering to
past practices, we believe orderly administration requires that precedent resolve any doubts." One wonders what case they envisage that will present a more
provocative challenge to consideration of the public
interest, and if past precedent in this case was sufficient for decision, why the immediate reference of
identical issues to the Congress for decision relating
to some unpredictable contingency in an unforesee-
able future?

And why, one may ask, does the urgency of seeking
refuge with the Congress arise only at this late date?
The commissioners were evidently aware of analo-
gous cases out of a long past, in which large business
concerns bought radio stations, while having and
maintaining a primary interest in other forms of
business. For they fill three pages with the listing of
them. Can it have been to bolster their courage as

against the doubts which "orderly administration requires precedent to resolve"?

More questions raise their troubling heads and we are left with the feeling that the public interest is not securely anchored in the Commission. The precedents of default and of timorous decision are too long and too many. A phrase of the minority commissioners interprets our feelings: "An administrative agency can defeat Congressional intent by avoiding its statutory responsibility as well as by exceeding its statutory authority." We are filled with an uneasy apprehension.

VII

The Midas Touch

ALL OF US can fairly criticize another man's actions. We can say we disagree with what he does and state our reasons. To impute motives is another matter altogether. This has to do with what a man is after. It is in general a dangerous, apart from being a most unpopular, pastime. Until quite recently any discussion of radio's philosophy would have suffered from this handicap. The motives which we attributed could have been denied by reference to statements made by the leaders of the industry. Their protestations of devotion to the public could have been used to sidestep the cold, unwelcome logic of the facts and the inductive arguments derived from them.

Today our argument no longer needs to rest on theory alone. Flushed with monetary success and confident in their power, spokesmen of radio are speaking out with a new and welcome candor. We now know from them what, in radio, makes Sammy run. The past is explained and what is in store for us is clearly foreshadowed. None of the statements that we shall quote have been denied. We can presume to have that evidence, for which we have groped by laborious analysis, straight from the horse's mouth.

We are indebted to a president of the National Association of Broadcasters for a revealing history of American radio. On May 16, 1945, Mr. J. Harold Ryan rose in Omaha, Nebraska, to address the Kiwanis Radio Week meeting. The spokesman of a great industry was on his feet.

Radio, past, present, and future, was his theme. For the past he had a passing, deprecatory word, spoken more in sorrow than in anger. "In the beginning," he said, "ownership of a radio station was considered to be a public philanthropy. . . . Money was required to operate stations, but in many cases the operators had a kind of 'artistic personality' which would not permit the acceptance of a gratuity [*sic*] except under the most dignified circumstances. Hence an advertiser was permitted to sponsor a program with bare mention of his name. . . . All was formality; individuality was ruled by restraint. . . . This kind of radio was strictly high hat, certainly not American, and was not destined to last."

But times, fortunately, improved, he said. Within a few years "many a station operator, who might have had a personal preference for poetry and the opera, learned some sound lessons in selling and merchandising under the tutelage of America's good, hardheaded businessmen, and it was the best thing that could have happened to him."

The speaker paused, as the audience watched the pale ghosts of a discredited past trail back into the limbo of forgetfulness — the philanthropist, the man with an "artistic personality" and "a personal preference for poetry and the opera," the man with "individuality ruled by restraint." "Certainly not American and not destined to last."

With a gesture suggesting the removal of cobwebs, the speaker recovered his contemporary poise. Addressing himself, with obvious relief, to the present, he continued: "Do you regard [radio] purely as a miracle, as a flash of inventive genius . . . or do you associate it with bookkeeping, clerks, secretaries, bank balances, customers, pay checks, and janitors?" The audience, obviously caught short by this grotesque association of ideas, offered no response. But the speaker provided his own answer. "American radio is the product of American business! It is just as much that kind of product as the vacuum cleaner, the washing machine, the automobile and the airplane . . . if the legend still persists that a radio station is some kind of an art center, a technical museum, or a little piece of Hollywood transplanted strangely to your home town, then the first official act of the second quarter century should be to list it along with the local dairies, laundries, banks, restaurants, and filling stations. . . ."

The reader deserves time out to rub his eyes and ask himself into what new wonderland he has been spirited by this imaginative and fluent gentleman. But we must hurry on. For the speaker later identifies for us a crucial date in radio's history.

"In 1935," he said, "radio and its advertisers really began to get together. Advertising agencies had learned how to produce successful programs with some degree of regularity." Not having a "personal preference for poetry" he didn't quote Shakespeare ("Let me not to the marriage of true minds admit impediments") to seal and sanctify this association. As a "good, hardheaded" businessman, he stuck to the vernacular — and let the cat out of the bag.

"In 1935 . . . radio and its advertisers really began to get together." We have observed, in previous chapters, something of what that beginning led to. It has taken ten years for a formulation of the philosophy to catch up with the practice which was the issue of this unforeseen liaison. It comes to us, in 1945, from the head of an advertising agency (the Duane Jones Company) which is said to place more than two thousand commercials on the air each week, through which twenty-six clients are said to sell approximately seventy-five million dollars' worth of packaged goods annually. Mr. Jones stated: —

"The best radio program is the one that sells the most goods, not necessarily the one that holds the highest Hooper or Crossley rating. . . . *No program can long endure that does not sell goods.* . . . We in the Duane Jones Company have found that, when we increase the length and number of commercials to test our programs, invariably their Crossley ratings go up. . . . When making these tests, we load the programs to the limit under NAB rulings with commercials that precede, interrupt, and follow these broadcasts. And we know from the results that *any arbitrary curtailment of commercials would seriously impair the audience value of these shows.*" This, then, we are given to understand, is the modern recipe for radio.

Lest the reader doubt Mr. Jones's right to bespeak his colleagues, let us quote another. The president of the American Tobacco Company is quoted in the *New York Times* of April 22, 1945, as follows: "We have some funny thinking here about radio, and we have been criticized for it. Taking 100 per cent as the total radio value, we give 90 per cent to commercials, to what's said for the product, and we give 10 per cent to the show. . . . We are commercial and we cannot afford to be anything else. I don't have the right to spend the stockholders' money just to entertain the public." This is a sound enough business principle. We look for no charity. But some will question whether business will thrive on radio if 90 per cent of its energy and thought goes to the "commercial" and 10 per cent to the program.

Radio's largest client is Procter & Gamble. According to *Broadcasting Magazine*, the firm spent some twenty-two million dollars on radio time and talent in 1944 alone. (This amount is four times the entire annual budget of the networks and stations operated by the Canadian Broadcasting Corporation.) The company contributes a further thought to the prevailing philosophy that dictates what we hear on the air. "P & G has a policy never to offend a single listener."

Commissioner Durr of the FCC provided a fitting comment on this policy when he said: "Never to offend anyone may be good salesmanship. But is it good radio? Is it good sense in times such as these in which we are living? The best in literature and drama, and even art and music, has offended. Milton offended in his time. So did Shakespeare and Victor Hugo in theirs. Tom Paine and Sam Adams and Jefferson and Hamilton and Madison and many more whose names we honor today did a lot of offensive speaking and writing in their time, but it was a time which required a challenge to greatness. . . . Out of their courage to offend came a Declaration of Independence and a Constitution and Bill of Rights."

We have, indeed, "some funny thinking here about radio." The English language and long-established concepts of value seem now to be subject to change. New and revolutionary ideas appear to be emerging. The "best" in what even Mr. Ryan admits to be an art is what sells goods. The meaning of progress has puzzled philosophers for centuries, but apparently the modern businessman has a simple yardstick for it in balance sheets. In the widest realm of communication yet made available to man, the ruling principle is "never to offend a single listener."

Writers, sickened by such conceptions of radio's role in our society, have in times past found refuge with the networks and the sanctuary of sustaining time. A remnant few still cleave to the sanctuary but, as we have seen, its floor space is diminishing, good sustaining time is at a discount. Nor are all networks still offering a refuge. Two years ago, the president of the National Broadcasting Company implicitly served notice on writers to submit to the control of the dollar philosophy or quit. "The argument," he said, "is now advanced that business control of broadcasting operations has nothing to do with program control. *This is to forget that 'he who controls the pocketbook controls the man.' Business control means complete control and there is no use arguing to the contrary."* [1]

Here, then, are the missing parts of the puzzle we have been piecing together, the motives that provide the clue to the practices we have examined. The networks' abdication to the advertisers, the relegation of sustaining programs to a subordinate role in program planning, the betrayal by local stations of the trust placed on them to serve their community, excesses in advertising, and the bias in handling controversial issues, are all explicable now. Radio has become the drudge of advertising, selling itself to big business for a handsome price, identified with it, body and soul, if any soul remains to it.

We have seen some of the consequences, for us. What radio has not yet seen is that its own food and sustenance is turning into gold, like Midas's food. *Variety* has lately published a long correspondence on the sterility of radio programs. Eddie Cantor and others have complained that radio's formula for entertainment is outworn, stereotyped, and that new talent is not encouraged.

Variety has also published an important article on

[1] Testimony to Senate Committee on Interstate Commerce, December 1943.

an exodus "without precedence" from radio to the legitimate theater of able writers. "For some time," it says, "the feeling has been mounting among many of the serious writers for radio that they have been retarded by a lack of freedom of expression . . . and that as long as radio remains more or less of a duplicating machine without encouraging creative expression and without establishing an identity of its own, it is inevitable that the guy who has something to say will seek other outlets." [2]

Variety is not alone in its concern. In the *New York Times* for July 15, 1945, one of radio's ablest writers, who received an award from the American Academy of Arts and Letters, Mr. Norman Rosten, summed up the situation in radio's most prosperous year as follows: —

> Most of us, including myself, who have worked in the media of poetry, drama, or the novel spheres in radio, know that radio is the sheerest caricature of art. . . . This is no snobbery. It is a fact and there are reasons. Imagine a painter working at his easel, say in a park. A man comes along, regards him for a moment, then approaches him and says cheerfully, "I don't know anything about painting, sir, but would you be so kind and put more red in your sunset. Just a bit more, if you please."

[2] *Variety*, June 20, 1945, "Top Scripting Talent Exodus" by George Rosen.

This kind of madness goes on in radio even more cheerfully and on a gargantuan scale. The man who wants more red in the sunset is the sponsor. He wants more love in the script. He wants a shorter scene. He wants a longer scene. He wants more action. He wants less action. Who is this sponsor? What are his qualifications? What is he doing in the writer's room, anyway, and why doesn't someone throw the gentleman out? . . . He is the man with the money. He belongs. *The sponsor and the advertising agency have taken over radio in this matter of right. . . . The broadcasting company sells Time.* It owns the air. It will sell you a piece. Period.

All art is an individual interpretation of experience. It is one man bringing forth a work solely his own, uniquely his own. In radio, uniformity is of utmost importance. Why? Well, for one thing, the writer in radio is faced with a highly censorable and very "public" audience which the sponsor feels he must placate at all costs. The writer in radio faces an audience whose prejudices and mores are so diverse that he is forced to get at the lowest common emotional denominator in order to please all. The problem is how to sell soap.

Radio writing, as it is now developed, is simply an adjunct of advertising. The word is fitted to the product. The product is god. The word is the interval between the announcements of god. We are nearing the middle of the twentieth century. Shall the singing commercial and the Lone Ranger inherit the earth?

All this, you may say, is beside the point. Perhaps the artist *should* have more scope. But after all, radio caters to the public and the public has no interest in art. Such a statement is a serious misreading of the evidence. As shown in case after case in previous chapters and as shown in quoted statements of business leaders, radio caters to the advertiser. It would like us to believe that, in so doing, it caters to the public too. Most of its public statements for more than a decade have been at pains to identify the public interest with the interests of big business. A great hoax has been put across, and it is time to expose the fact. Hard thinking is involved, but it is worth the effort.

Commercial radio, it is claimed, gives the public what it wants. "Giving the public what it wants" is a form of verbal sleight of hand. The slickness of the phrase deceives the ear. We have only to pause and ask ourselves what "the public" is, to recognize the fiction. You can think of the public in different ways. If you want to be literal, it can be defined as the totality of people, or, in terms of radio, the totality of radio-set owners. It remains to be proved that the total radio audience has *any* single common *interest*. Interest in news is perhaps the nearest approximation.

Or you can think of the public as the great majority of people. This is already an exclusive definition. It excludes the minority. Thus, according to this definition, the area of common interests is automatically reduced. The majority of listeners can be confidently said to have a broad common interest in entertainment. But this is only true in a sense so broad as already to mean very little. The factor of individual taste and preference now enters into the equation. Different people will like different kinds of entertainment. A fragmentation has set in to modify the concept of a totality of common interest. We must bear in mind, also, that this definition of a majority public is already totally exclusive of a minority, the size of which we cannot estimate.

Fragmentation of a different kind has also to be reckoned with. Even among a supposed majority of all listeners the desire, say, for entertainment will not always be simultaneous. Nor will the desire be coextensive (not everyone will want as much entertainment for as long a period of time). The competitive zeal of radio to exploit a new hit with the public (quiz programs, the current craze for crime detection stories, and thriller dramas for children, for example) thus does a disservice, even to the majority public, by providing an overdose of a single kind of entertainment. A majority of the majority is now getting preferential treatment, thus swelling the minority.

If you exclude half a dozen top-ranking radio programs, this process of fragmentation (resulting from variants in the nature, extent, and incidence of common interests) increases progressively as you try to define common denominators of public taste; you are forced, in fact, to the conclusion that this is a misleading and illusory kind of definition of what "the public" is. Let us attempt a better one.

What Is the Public?

The term "public" is an abstraction — like the definition of a line (as something without height or breadth). You cannot draw a line that conforms to the definition. Nor can you identify the public any more closely than you can draw a line. But, as in the definition of a line, you can define its distinctive attributes. The distinctive attribute of the radio public is that it is an organic whole. It consists of individual organic parts. The public is the sum of these organic parts. Service to the public thus involves service to each and all of its separate organic units. There is no other way of doing it. Attend to the parts, and the whole takes care of itself.

But these organic units differ in size and in kind and in significance as far as their common element is concerned — their interests and tastes. From a social point of view, some of these units of interest are more significant than others. From a cultural point of view, others have primary importance. From a political point of view, others, and so on right down the list. This raises the difficult question as to whether they should be catered to, programwise, in strict arithmetical proportion to their size.

The radio industry says yes. Minorities should get time on the air proportionate to their size. A tenth of the time should be given to good music, say, if a tenth of the public is known to appreciate good music. The barometer of public interest will and should show the level of interest, in this program or that, to be provided for.

Apart from the question (which we won't beg now) that our statistics on who likes what are far from adequate (the barometer isn't reliable), and the fact that, even according to available statistics, minorities are not catered to in proportion to their numbers (interest in labor problems is only one of many examples that might be cited), this contention deserves careful study before we let it pass.

This argument carries the implication that all interests are equivalent in value or significance. There is a very strong presumption that this was not the thought of those who drafted the law for broadcasting. The

term "public interest," as used in the Radio and Communications Acts defining the service function of all
radio stations, embraces a much broader concept of
interest than mere program popularity. In intention it
approximates more nearly the concept of public welfare, or the general good of the people.

It is at this point that the radio executive throws
up his hands in horror. "Do you mean to tell me," he
protests, "that *I* am to decide what's good for other
people? Am *I* my brother's keeper?" Have we a
twentieth-century answer to Cain's question?

The first director-general of the British Broadcasting Corporation had his pat and ready. Radio, he
claimed, should give the public, not what it likes, but
what it ought to like. For more than ten years the
British public swallowed Sir John Reith's recipe for
what he thought they ought to like. It was not in
itself a bad recipe. Owing to wave-length restrictions
in Europe, Britain before the war had, in effect, only
two program services to choose from. Entertainment
programs and "cultural" programs had approximately
fifty-fifty representation, light and serious programs
being juxtaposed on the two program services with a
slight bias in favor of entertainment. Minorities got
just about as much program service as the majority.
There was entertainment almost all the time, but no
choice of entertainment. You chose between light and

serious, or between light and darkness, as some felt.

It is quite possible that the result of Sir John Reith's policy has been the more rapid development in Britain than with us of increased interest in quite a large number of social and cultural subjects. He enjoined among other things an austere observance of the Sabbath Day. There were no jazz bands, no comedy. Here again, virtue may have resulted. But assume even a perfect recipe for what is good for people. Assume an E for excellence in people's adaptation to such a prefabricated formula for self-improvement. Still, somehow, one's gorge rises. There is arrogance in the assumption that any one man knows, or even has any business finding out by himself, what is good for others, particularly when that one man heads a radio monopoly. This isn't free air we breathe. There is a sultriness, as of fascist authoritarianism, in the offing. One's democratic stomach turns. For the author's money, he would prefer (without intending blasphemy) to go to hell on his own steam than to appear thus in heaven under escort. Freedom involves the responsibility of choice. Americans don't want any loading of the scales of choice. Being one's brother's keeper on such terms is not for us.

Radio's spokesmen and practitioners have made it plain that the advantage they seek is profits. This is nothing to quarrel about. Our quarrel is with their trespassing on the advantage of others. Radio is its brother's keeper to the extent of fostering and furthering the public advantage from which its private advantage derives. Its error is in a misconception of wherein the public advantage lies and of posing a false antithesis between the theories of Sir John Reith and the BBC and the American theory of broadcasting. Radio's spokesmen have misinterpreted the American theory and by doing so have laid themselves open to the most damaging of all charges — that of being undemocratic. This is so serious a charge as to require convincing substantiation.

Our American system of broadcasting provides its own safeguard against the main defect of British and of government-controlled radio monopoly. No one man, no network even, can determine what the public is to hear. By establishing a competitive system we have, in theory at least, provided not an alibi for, but a distribution of, public responsibility. The lawmakers relied on qualities that in the past have distinguished American private enterprise — initiative, imagination, a readiness to take risks — to give us the widest diversification of program service. At all levels, local, regional, and national, competition would, it was believed, give us this richness and diversity of choice.

We have seen how, at all levels, this expected diversity has been progressively curtailed. In this chapter we have seen why. The dollar philosophers offer us a theory of radio program policy which is at once an insult to the intelligence and a menace to the public interest. Monopoly, thrown out the front door, comes in by the back door and in a far more dangerous guise. The radio industry aligned with and subordinated to big-business advertisers becomes simply an adjunct of advertising. The word is fitted to the product. The product is god. The word is the interval between the announcements of god. We know, from Mr. Ryan, the date of this fantastic transformation. We have ten years of distorted thinking to make good.

The American theory of distributed responsibility absolves any man in radio from asking himself if he is his brother's keeper. But he has only to exercise his own intelligence to emancipate himself entirely from the burden of prescribing for others. The formula is simple. It is the reverse of Mr. Ryan's contemptuous dismissal of other people's "personal preferences" to crave room for his own crude and insulting estimate of public interests. He has only to cast his eye over the known and observable activities and interests of thousands of individuals and groups to discover a range of subject matter that will tax the ingenuity even of a man whose task is to communicate sixteen hours a day 365 times a year. Provision for these interests, some vast and some more limited in their extent, need be at no one's expense (not even the advertiser's). Majority interests can still be amply catered for. We have plenty of networks and stations to provide variety of choice — if the radio industry will stop chasing its own tail.

In an earlier chapter, we listed five broad categories of interest that radio might reasonably cater for. Provision for these five alone would more than fill the program charts of all the stations in America. Thanks to Mr. Ryan and his fellow spokesmen, we know why most of these categories are not being adequately catered for. They are not regarded as good (that is, according to radio's philosophy, paying) vehicles for advertising copy. Radio thinks it has discovered a "safe" formula for selling soap. There are those who believe that it is far from safe, and that, in fact, the copy is getting ragged at the edges and badly thumbed from excessive circulation. Mr. Cantor, thinking of radio entertainment, and Mr. Rosten, thinking of the artist in words, are at one on this. But let that pass. Since when, we may ask, has American free enterprise played safe? Where have the daring initiative and the readiness to take risks gone? Who are these men who equate public interest in radio with low sales resistance? They are men, blinded by their dollar philosophy both to the true character of the average American and to their own best interests, who reckon in strictly cash terms. Their philosophy has affected their vision until it is so narrow that they can look down the neck of a bottle with both eyes at once. They have demonstrated both in word and in deed that they lack faith in mankind. They take us for what we are and not for what we have it within us to become. This is not only undemocratic. It is un-American, as a brief résumé of our nation's development will show.

Material success and a high idealism are two outstanding characteristics for which America is known and respected throughout the world. For the achievement of material success we have a formula, marked clearly on the bottle — "Made in America." The growth of our republic and of our social mores may be said to stem largely from a belief in two basic necessities for a full and virile way of life — self-reliance and opportunity. The self-made man, the man who has pulled himself up by his own boot straps, is not a unique American type, but he is distinctively American. From log cabin to White House represents an American kind of idealism and we count with pride the number of those who, in our history, have thus made the grade. Private enterprise, we have believed, provides the opportunity for the fullest exercise of that self-reliance which our children are raised to respect and emulate. This is the formula for the material side of our success.

But this is not the whole of American history. Equally typical and distinctive is the American belief in education. We have (or at least we have had) a passion for it. Without being too clear about what education means, we have always entertained the notion that material success is not in itself enough. It leaves a void, a feeling of incompleteness. Our idealism remains unsatisfied. We have built, as it were, great mansions, only to realize that, however large and luxuriously appointed, they are inadequate without a view, a landscape at the door with expansive and satisfying vistas. The key to the door we believe to be education. Beyond the door is a landscape that we cannot describe, but long to view.

The spread of education is not only important in itself, from a social and a democratic point of view; it is essential to the economic future of our radio executive. If he wants continuing profits, he must contribute, and handsomely, to the furtherance of education. Consider an analogy.

The manufacture, in ever greater quantities, of an increasing variety of goods, and the creation of widespread markets for them, are what spells economic prosperity. A like continuing expansion of the horizons of people's *interests* is equally necessary if radio is not to face diminishing returns on its present overly restricted line of goods which is its range of program services.

New economic markets are created. They do not happen. New horizons of interest are likewise created by the good old American practice of providing opportunity. There is a limit to where you can get in pulling yourself up by your own boot straps. In the end, you need a ladder. Education is the never-ending ladder of nonmaterial opportunity. Radio has been busy these many years tearing out all but the bottom rungs. So far from creating opportunity, it has been doing much to retard the expansion of our interests, if not to stop it dead in its tracks. How and why should be plain enough from previous pages. As a former commissioner of the FCC put it, ten years ago, "To anyone who studies the situation from the inside there is (in radio) quite evident a contempt for educational and cultural influences that is most unusual to any scientific field of development." [3] The reason for this contempt is clear. These influences failed to respond immediately to the Midas touch.

Herein lies the tragedy of radio's wayward progress. We have a sound system, the soundest in the world in its safeguards against radio's greatest men-

[3] Commissioner Payne in 1936.

ace — thought control. We gave private enterprise a free rein to develop this medium of hope, enrichment, and expanded opportunity. Where have they driven it? Up to the gates of Midas's palace. Thought control kills independence of mind — the self-reliance that we cherish. But the Midas touch is the kiss of death to opportunity. Self-reliance and opportunity, material and nonmaterial, the two together have made America great. Admitting to a marked preference for poetry and the opera, but an even more marked preference for our neighbor and his right, and infinite capacity for self-development, let us offer Mr. Ryan "some sound lessons in selling and merchandising" the only commodity that insures him a continuously expanding market.

We must go back, for a start, to our redefinition of "the radio public." It consists, as we saw, of individuals with a variety of group interests. The only dish to serve up to such a public is one that satisfies the tastes of all these separate groups. Radio's business is, then, to serve a very good stew. Mr. Ryan's recipe for stew has too few ingredients and too much pepper. Too much pep destroys the individual flavors. The best recipe involves a judicious blending of individual flavors without smothering one by another. We should get a stew more to the general taste if radio observed such principles as the following: —

1. The business of radio is to expose us continuously to new and more varied interests. It is good business to do so. Radio thus spreads its risks. Any single appetite gets sated. Certainly the capacity to satisfy it runs out eventually.

But new interests, like flowers, grow only by exposure to the light. It is ignorance that keeps us in the dark. All of us (to take one example only) are, or can be made, interested in our neighbors, their activities, and their way of looking at things. Even here in America, we have an interest in and understanding of one another to acquire which is still dangerously undeveloped. But our neighbors today are our fellow citizens throughout the world. It will be a long time before we get to know them and we shall need continuous exposure.

2. Some interests develop more slowly than others. Any educator knows this. The cultivation of such interests, therefore, involves prolonged exposure. To use a metaphor, such a flowering of the mind and sensibilities, once it takes place, produces blooms that endure longer and are more highly prized than the quick-growing weeds of superficial interest. Interest in the arts is an example. Radio, to its credit, has fostered a widespread interest in music. It took time, but it has proved a continuing asset. The interest does not flag and is still underfed. The longer the

exposure the greater the interest. It is a sound business principle to invest part of your capital in long-
term securities. Radio's current capital is overinvested
in short-term program stock.

3. There is no short cut to the flowering of either
the mind or the imagination. Again, to use a garden-
ing metaphor, planters are warned against the use of
artificial fertilizers. Either the plant dies or it comes
up with heightened and distorted hues. "The mind is
its own place." Salesmen have, or think they have, a
basic recipe for selling goods. The promotion of intellectual interests is not like the promotion of goods.
The mass production of dairies, laundries, and restaurants has nothing to do with the case.

The cultivation of interest requires not only time
but talent and a wide variety of talents. Radio is not
a duplicating machine. No one technique of program
production suffices. No two writers write alike. It is a
mistake to try to make them do so. The honest product of a writer's pen does not need to be tricked out
with embellishments, jazzed up, least of all stream-
lined. Individuality is rare enough to be in great public demand. Radio can afford to take risks with it.

4. Maturity of outlook and judgment is not a hot-
house product. It is an all-weather plant, sturdy and
proof against shocks. The greater the exposure, the
sturdier the plant. It is thus that we acquire the indi-

viduality ruled by restraint which Mr. Ryan resents so much.

We shall not achieve maturity as a people if radio's policy is never to offend a single listener. There are many listeners who need to be offended, in the name of Christianity, democracy, and our own Bill of Rights. Freedom of speech involves the right to offend and be offended. America can take it.

5. The educator (and the champion of democracy) has an infinite respect for individuality. The belief is rooted in practical experience, not in sentiment. The growth of individuality is fostered by encouraging its strengths and not by indulging its weaknesses. Radio has too often indulged human weaknesses — credulity and lethargy — for the ulterior motive of selling more goods. This kind of indulgence is a social menace, a crime against democracy and an offense against American respect for individuality. It makes instruments of individuals. The listener is not for use. The sentiment expressed in several of our quotations from industry spokesmen reflect an attitude to people that is contemptible because it bespeaks contempt.

Radio executives should read *Hamlet:* "Why, look you now, how unworthy a thing you make of me! You would play upon me; you would seem to know my stops; you would pluck out the heart of my mystery; you would sound me from the lowest note to the top of my compass: and there is much music, excellent voice, in this little organ; yet cannot you make it speak. 'Sblood, do you think I am easier to be played on than a pipe? Call me what instrument you will, though you can fret me, yet you cannot play upon me." Perhaps we ought to add, at least you do so at your peril.

Before concluding this chapter we must forestall a possible misapprehension. We have had hard words to say. We believe them, on the evidence, to be justified. But no universal condemnation of radio's performance is intended. It has, on many sides, a magnificent record. There are many men and women in the industry who do not subscribe to the policies propounded by some of its leaders. We should like to think that we speak in their defense. The system, as we have repeatedly insisted, is sound. Radio has taken a wrong turn but the return journey is not barred. What we have tried to demonstrate is that the public interest and reasonable profits, so far from being incompatible, are inextricably interlinked. The fostering of wider educational opportunity, with due regard for the intricacy and delicacy of the lock, opens the door not only to a fuller democratic life, but to the only certain prospect of continuing returns on radio's investment of enterprise and of imagination. The future prosperity of the radio industry depends on a broader and more enlightened sense of social responsibility and a less cynical belief in what each of us has it within him to become.

There will emerge, in time, a philosophy of radio which freely recognizes that radio's interests are best served by distributive responsibility, not only within the industry, but outside of it. The voice of the public in radio, as in industry at large and in democracy as a whole, must emerge as a contributory and, on any fundamental issue, decisive voice. (In a later chapter we shall discuss how, in radio, this can be progressively achieved.) But as long as the public lacks its own direct and effective means of voicing its collective will, guardianship by an agency of government is entailed. We have such an agency in the Federal Communications Commission. In the next chapter we shall explain its role and try to account for its failure in preventing, in good time, the serious abuses in which, as we have seen, the radio industry has indulged to the detriment of public interest and its own good name.

VIII

Washington's No. 1
Whipping Boy – the FCC

THE FEDERAL Communications Commission had, until 1941, rarely made the headlines. In 1941, it did.

It was the month of May. It was very hot. The scene was the annual convention of the National Association of Broadcasters. The pundits of the radio industry were in mass assembly. By special invitation, Mr. James Lawrence Fly, then chairman of the FCC, was a "guest" in the audience. As it turned out, he was *the* audience. The speaker at the rostrum was Mark Ethridge, one-time president of the Association. His speech was long, indignant, and abusive. He flayed the Commission and its chairman, with a tongue as biting as a whiplash. The FCC, he said, has "gone beyond any powers conferred in the law . . . has been prejudiced and frequently punitive."

We're well on the way, he claimed, to government ownership of radio.

Mr. Fly flushed. As the speech ended, he half rose, as though to speak, but the conference chairman's quick eye spotted him. He adjourned the conference. Next day, Mr. Fly summoned the press and made a statement. Radio's management, he told them, "reminds me of a dead mackerel in the moonlight which both shines and stinks." A servant of the government had spoken back. Reporters rushed to the phone booths. The press awarded him the accolade of banner headlines.

This incident is unique only in the lurid choice of language by a government official to rebut a heated and damaging charge. Before and since, the FCC has been abused and accused of "star chamber proceedings," of "terroristic control," of dictatorial powers amounting, as Mr. William S. Paley, president of the Columbia Broadcasting System, put it to a Senate committee, to "regulation by the raised eyebrow." Hardly a single year has passed since the FCC was established in 1934 without a motion in the House or Senate to investigate its actions.[1] No agency of government in recent years has been such a continuing storm center.

[1] Resolutions to investigate the FCC were moved in Congress in 1934, 1936, 1937, 1938, 1939, 1940, 1941, and 1942.

Radio's first regulatory agency, as we have earlier seen, was born "out of" chaos "by" public indignation. These ill-assorted parents quickly died. Chaos and indignation subsided. Their child, the Federal Radio Commission, born with the passage of the Radio Act of 1927, was handed over to foster parents, to the Congress. This orphan child was first starved (the Congress, while passing the Radio Act, voted no funds with which the Commission could carry on!), then fed a diet sufficient to sustain life but inadequate for full or continuing existence. For seven years the Commission survived on a year-to-year basis, subject to annual renewal of its powers. Only in 1934 was it conceded permanent status. By an act of Congress — the Communications Act — it was then rechristened the Federal Communications Commission and received grudgingly into the bosom of the family.

Starved at birth and neglected in infancy, it grew up to be a timid child, subject to rare but alarming bursts of frustrated rage, uncertain of its rights. Constantly harried by its foster parents, it was given quite inadequate guidance on deportment. It was just told to do good and when it tried to apply this broad moral precept it was roundly abused, year in, year out, and told that it was vicious, grasping, undisciplined, and untrustworthy. When it ventured out into the world, it was cold-shouldered by its cousin, John Public, and bullied by a well-organized gang of older boys, the radio industry, with strong muscles and abusive tongues, and defied when it asserted itself.

If such a picture hardly squares with the conventional conception of tyrannical bureaucracy, it only shows the gulf that currently exists (and gets assiduously dredged by interested parties) between popular fictions about government agencies and the real facts.

The Powers of the FCC

The main duties of the Commission are, broadly speaking, threefold: —

1. To assign wave lengths in such a way as to bring a satisfactory radio signal to the largest number of listeners. This is a technical and extremely complicated matter which we can best leave to the experts. Though it affects us as listeners, the solution of this problem appears to be near with the advent of FM broadcasting.

2. To grant temporary licenses to radio stations to operate "in the public interest, convenience or necessity" and to renew the license if the public interest has been served. We should underscore in our minds the temporary nature of the license granted,

for it recalls to us *our* interests and rights and duties in radio. The license is temporary because the air belongs to the people. As a distinguished lawyer has put it, "the broadcaster has only the tenuous right of a tenant at will."

3. The Commission is responsible for determining the desirable over-all balance and content of program service and for a general review, at the time for renewal of licenses, of the kind of program service rendered by a station. The test of service rendered is the public interest.

The Act gives little guidance to the Commission as to what constitutes satisfactory program service. It forbids obscene or profane language, and publicity for lotteries, and it insists that equal facilities be provided by a station to all qualified political candidates for office. For the rest, the Commission must formulate and apply its own standards, subject to two cautions only: its findings must not be arbitrary or capricious and it must not censor programs. That is, it must not pass judgment on a program in advance of its being broadcast, or do anything which interferes with the right of free speech.

This duty to review the program service proposed by an applicant for a radio license, or an existing station's past program service, is by far the most important function of the Commission. Some spokesmen of the radio industry have contended that it doesn't exist, and that the Act intended merely that the Commission concern itself with the technical aspects of radio — with assigning wave lengths and seeing that stations adhere to them. The question of satisfactory program service can be settled, they say, between the industry and the listening public.[2] Government interference is superfluous and undesirable, is, in fact, censorship. The Commission is just a traffic cop responsible for seeing that the traffic sticks to the right lane and observes the stop-go signs, not responsible at all for where the traffic goes — that is, the destination to which it carries its passengers. This is far too important a question to allow of any lingering doubt in anybody's mind as to what the law's intention really is.

If the Commission were really limited to purely technical considerations, one might reasonably argue

---

[2] The Commission answered this contention as long as seventeen years ago. "Listeners have no protection unless it is given to them by this Commission, for they are powerless to prevent the ether waves carrying unwelcome messages from entering the walls of their houses. Their only alternative, which is not to tune in on the station, is not satisfactory, particularly when in a city such as Erie only the local stations can be received during a large part of the year. When a station is misused . . . the entire listening public is deprived of the use of a station for a service in the public interest." Federal Radio Commission, in the matter of stations WRAK, WABF, WBRE, and WMBS, August 29, 1928.

that its members should be technicians, engineers, and radio experts. In actual fact, the Commission has rarely had more than one such technical expert among its members. Moreover, it is quite clear that the original sponsors of the Act had other purposes than purely technical decisions in mind for the Commission. Senator Dill, for instance, sponsor of both the Radio Act of 1927 and the Communications Act of 1934, had this to say about Commission personnel: —

> I think it should be composed of men who have an understanding of the public needs, men of vision and great ability who will administer this law from the standpoint of the public interest and particularly with a view to the future development of the radio art for the social and economic good of our people. . . . I do not think it would be wise to have a Commission made up of technical experts because technical experts would not take the big view and the broad view and have the vision which I think the members of the Commission ought to have.[3]

The big view and the broad view and the vision. For what? For "the future development of the radio *art* for the social and economic good of our people." The intention seems clear enough.

It would, of course, have been easier for all con-

[3] 67 *Congressional Record* 12358.

cerned had the Act of 1934 defined more exactly what kind of program service was in the public interest. Stations would have been forewarned and the Commission could have applied the letter of the law. But Congress saw clearly that no such definition was either possible or desirable. Radio was in its infancy and public interest is anyhow subject to variant interpretation as times and circumstances change. Though the Act could have been improved in many respects, it would have been madness to put radio programing in such a strait jacket. Instead, the Congress appointed a permanent regulatory Commission and delegated to it discretion to interpret the meaning of public interest, convenience, or necessity.

While not explicitly so stated in the Act, there are strong grounds for concluding that Congress intended this discretion to cover program service. For it must be remembered that the Communications Act of 1934 was not the first attempt to legislate for radio. The Radio Act of 1927 preceded it by seven years. The substantive provisions of the Communications Act were substantial or identical re-enactments of the previous Radio Act. Both acts had the same sponsors in the House and Senate. The original Federal Radio Commission was, as we have seen, created for a term of one year only. In each successive Congress, between 1927 and

1932, members of the Commission appeared before Congressional committees. Congress was thus fully informed as to its activities and its interpretation of its powers, and these powers had frequently been held by the Commission to include the refusal to re-new a station's license on the grounds of unsatisfactory program service. Several such cases had occurred before 1934 and the Congress knew about them. Thus, at hearings in March 1934,[4] the Chairman of the Commission replied to a question as to whether the Commission had any right to pass on the quality of programs broadcast: —

> We do not pretend to tell the stations at all what they can or cannot broadcast. It is only after these broadcasts have taken place when we come to pass on the question of public interest, convenience or necessity. Then we are permitted . . . to take into consideration the public service of that particular station.

Although informed of this interpretation and of others in similar vein, Congress re-enacted, in 1934, in identical language, the censorship and free-speech provision of the Act of 1927. In other words, the Federal Radio Commission had established prece-

[4] Hearings on the McFadden Amendment, March 1934, p. 191.

dent after precedent which justified Commission action based on program review. The Congress knew of these precedents and did not demur. There is, therefore, a strong presumption that when Congress was clearly informed through its committee members as to the Commission's own interpretation of its powers, and neither criticized nor legislated to change or overrule them, it intended to adopt those interpretations in the Act of 1934.

But this is not all. The courts also sustained the right of the Commission to consider the character and quality of program service as an essential aspect of public interest. Many cases involving program issues have been before the courts, but so far no principle of regulation established by the Commission has been overruled. In a number of cases the lower court acknowledged program considerations to be relevant even in cases decided primarily on other grounds.[5] On two occasions the court supported the Commission when refusal to renew a license was based solely on past program performance.[6] And eventually the Supreme Court itself approved, in the

[5] *Federal Radio Commission* v. *Nelson Brothers*, 289 U.S. 77; *Ansley* v. *FRC*, 47 F (2d) 600; *Chicago Federation of Labor* v. *FRC*, 41 F (2d) 427; *Evangelical Lutheran Synod* v. *FCC*, 105 F (2d) 793, etc.

[6] *KFKB* v. *FRC*, 47 F (2d) 670; *Trinity Methodist Church* v. *FRC*, 62 F (2d) 850, *cert. den.* 284, U.S. 599; 288 U.S. 599.

famous Sanders case, the Commission's right to consider program performance.

Finally, the radio industry itself, speaking through the mouthpiece of the National Association of Broadcasters, has supported the Commission. In hearings before the Committee on Interstate Commerce in the House in 1934, their statement included the following: —

> It is the manifest duty of the licensing authority in passing on applications for licenses, or the renewal thereof, to determine whether or not the applicant is rendering or can render an adequate public service. Such service necessarily includes broadcasting of a considerable proportion of programs devoted to education, religion, labor, agricultural and similar activities concerned with human betterment. In actual practice over a period of seven years . . . this has been the principal test which the Commission has applied. . . .

The right of the Commission to pass judgment on past program service is thus clearly established. What, then, is all the commotion about? Has the Commission usurped such power? Has it in fact been arbitrary and capricious? Once again, let us look at the facts.

The power of the Commission most resented and most feared by the radio industry is the power to revoke or refuse renewal of a station's license. How often has it been exercised? Between 1934 and 1942 the Commission revoked exactly two licenses and refused to renew thirteen. In only a single case have the grounds for revocation had to do with program service. The rest have been cases of fraudulent misrepresentation, technical violations, failure to offer testimony, or other types of default. The only case concerned with programs involved "the constant and repeated broadcasting of false, fraudulent and misleading medical advertisement, sale of worthless stock over the air, and so on." [7]

The revocation of a license is admittedly an extreme act, a last resort not to be used without due warning. An agency judged capable of "regulation by the raised eyebrow" can afford to stop short of extremities of action. How often has the eyebrow lifted upward? The Commission registered objection to a Mae West program in 1938; it denounced the "Men from Mars" program (wise only after the event, as were the rest of us, to the amazing possibilities of panic latent in a piece of imaginative make-believe). The rest is, virtually, silence.

The most heinous "crime" of the Commission was

[7] These facts are taken from Hearings before the House Committee on Interstate and Foreign Commerce, H. R. 5497 (1942), Part III, p. 86.

its Chain Broadcasting Report (product, incidentally, of pressure on the Commission by a Congress nervous about monopoly control in radio). The industry used every device in its power to have the report quashed. They warned that it meant the end of our American system of broadcasting.[8] They fought it through the lower courts and on up to the Supreme Court. The Supreme Court sustained the Commission, and five deadly words by Associate Justice Frankfurter silenced at long last the contention that the FCC had no right of control over program service. The law, said the Supreme Court Justice, places on the Commission the burden of deciding "the composition of the traffic." Months of arduous labor went to the drafting of this report. Millions of words were filed in protesting briefs. And the result? A moral victory, a victory of principle, but with limited practical results.

To the Chain Broadcasting Report we are indebted for the Blue Network (now the American Broadcasting Company) as a network independent of RCA control. (RCA previously controlled both

[8] The Supreme Court comments nicely on this kind of threat. "It is the history of monopolies, in this country and in England, that predictions of ruin are habitually made by them when it is attempted, by legislation, to restrain their operations and to protect the public. . . ." (*Northern Securities Co.* v. *U.S.*, 193 U.S. 197, 351.)

the Blue and the Red networks of NBC.) The risk of monopoly in radio was to this extent diminished. Whether the listener also gained the theoretical advantage of increased competition (in better and more varied programs) the reader must judge for himself. A comparison of programs on the Blue, then and now, repays the trouble of such study.

The report also gave us what in theory, at any rate, is a great gain. Where, in a given locality, an affiliated station does not choose to carry a program offered by its network, another station may take up the option. Thus, for example, if for Raymond Swing a local affiliate of the ABC decided to substitute a local program, another station in that locality could carry him. Networks previously had refused their programs to any but their own affiliated stations. The Commission, with its chain broadcasting regulations, thus scored an important point of principle. It was a victory for the listener. Unfortunately, the number of cases in which this option has been taken up, since the regulations were enforced, is negligible. The Commission labored greatly and brought forth a mouse.

Apart from these activities, one searches the reports and findings of the Commission in vain for evidence of either strong leadership or courageous action. Congress and the radio industry, with their

constant vituperations, have created the fiction of
a monster. Stripped of this sensational verbal cloth-
ing, the Commission emerges as the timid, fractious
child of our fable. Its record, judged by high standards of the public interest, is by and large one of
default, not of capricious or arbitrary action. In support of our contention, let us again appeal to facts.

1. *Failure to revoke a license despite fraudulent
representation.* We have noted in previous chapters
a series of unhappy developments and trends in radio which bring discredit on a system of broadcasting that we believe to be the best in the world. Not
one of these excesses has been effectively tackled by
the Commission. We have not, however, mentioned
one aspect of the problem that equally affects the
good name of the industry and is vital to the public interest — the moral integrity of applicants for
radio licenses.

In the files of the FCC, there are numerous instances in which, after a hearing, it has been found
that an applicant has misrepresented material facts,
or, to speak plainly, has lied to the Commission. Despite this, the Commission has renewed their licenses. Thus, in the case of Station WTMC, Ocala,
Florida, and Station WALP, Panama City, Florida,
the Commission recently found that it had been
"grossly misled" and that the deception (conceal-

ment of the "real party in interest") was deliberate. Yet the licenses of these two stations were renewed.[9]

Similarly, Stations KTBC, Austin, Texas; KNET, Palestine, Texas; KRBA, Lufkin, Texas; KSAM, Huntsville, Texas; KGKB, Tyler, Texas; and KGFI, Brownsville, Texas, were found either to have secured a license through false and fraudulent representations regarding their financing and ownership or to have been transferred without the Commission's consent.[10] Yet their licenses were not revoked. The main reason for extending the license period to three years was to allow a more careful review of pledges made and service rendered. Despite this, renewal of licenses has continued to be largely perfunctory. Small wonder, therefore, that station licensees have come to regard their right to an assigned frequency as permanent, rather than as "the tenuous right of a tenant at will."

2. *Failure to revoke licenses despite inadequate program service in the public interest.* We have already examined one case (Station WMFG, Hibbing, Minnesota) where failure to serve the local community might seem to have warranted at least a mild

[9] Panama City Broadcasting Company, Inc., 9 FCC 208 (1942); Ocala Broadcasting Company, Inc., 9 FCC 223 (1942).

[10] Red Lands Broadcasting Association, *et al.*, 8 FCC 4731479 (1941).

protest by the Commission. The even more flagrant case of Station KIEV, Glendale, California, likewise illustrates the Commission's past record of inactivity. These are not isolated examples. Their number, in fact, is legion. Principles of program service, enunciated by the Commission, have again and again been flouted by the radio industry, but this has passed without action — often even without comment by the Commission.

It was not until 1945 that the Commission gave any public sign of even being conscious of this rubber-stamp endorsement of default. On April 10, 1945, it did, at last, announce "a policy of more detailed review of broadcast station performance when passing upon applications for license renewals." [11] Decision on the application of a number of stations was deferred and a questionnaire was issued asking some very relevant questions on apparent disparities between their promise and performance.

3. *Failure to adjust principles of program operation to changed times and circumstances.*

We have already noted important changes in both the art and the organization of radio. Transcriptions have come into their own; networks have radically modified the function and operation of local stations; radio advertising has become economically

[11] FCC News Release No. 81575.

significant (aside from its cultural effects) beyond anything foreseen in early days. In these and similar instances of change, a lead might have been expected from the Commission — a revised statement of policy, of principles governing its decisions.

Here, again, default is the outstanding aspect of its performance. From the start the principles of broadcasting policy and practice have depended to a considerable extent on precedents created by the Commission, based on "the big view, the broad view and vision." The listener's interests have become increasingly precarious as the radio industry consolidated its powers and its prestige, perfected its lobbying techniques. The listener, to this day unorganized and therefore inadequately represented, could look only to the Commission for guardianship. The record suggests that "the hungry sheep look up and are not fed."

4. *Failure to define basic principles of program planning*. But the main default of the Commission, chief cause perhaps of its unhappy relations with the industry, is its failure in eleven years ever to define in broad, clear terms what type of over-all program service it judged to be in the public interest, convenience, or necessity. A great injustice has here been done to the radio industry. The Commission holds the power of life or death over radio stations. The

least that could be asked of it is a clear statement of what crimes involve the death penalty. The "fear of the unknown," as one operator said, has hung like the sword of Damocles over their heads. Little wonder that they feel, as another put it, that "the broadcasters of this country are under a compulsion that is invisible."

By its occasional inept and capricious (because inconstant) strictures on specific programs, the Commission has kept radio on tenterhooks as to when and where the next blow might fall. The latent power of the Commission, far more than its actual exercise of power, has created a nervousness and uncertainty that has done little to "encourage the larger and more effective use of the radio" which the Communications Act prescribed as among the Commission's functions.

Worse still, by the timidity it has shown in failing to check abuses, by its perfunctory and all but automatic renewal of licenses, it has led many to conclude that they could get away with murder. Definition by the FCC of such basic program categories as we have suggested earlier, broad as they are, would at least have put stations on notice as to the *kind* of program balance expected of them. Hibbing and Glendale and hundreds of like stations would have known, and known in advance, the *general* type and range of interests and issues to be provided for. No definition of the *amount* of time to be given any specified subject would be practicable or desirable, or for that matter necessary. The Commission must always exercise judgment. That is its function.

But without a yardstick to measure by or to refer to, no valid body of precedents can be established, no judgment can seem other than capricious to the victim, nor can there be any stable development of radio's program services. We have seen (in the last chapter, on radio's philosophy) why program policy cannot be left to the discretion of the industry alone; seen also what happens to the public interest when, in effect, it is so left. There is a lot of lost ground to be regained. The public interest will remain unserved until the Commission interprets in broad clear terms the current meaning of a phrase in which still lies concealed the future destiny of radio's service to America.

It is obviously undesirable and inexcusable for the Commission to insist arbitrarily either on the amount of time to be devoted to any subject or on the quality of specific programs broadcast — except in extreme and obvious cases of default. Any attempt at narrow definition will defeat itself. To demand, for example, that time be reserved for educational programs will achieve nothing. What *is* educational?

But the Commission can define, and insist on provision for, such general categories as we proposed in Chapter III. It can decide whether, in its judgment, *each and all* of these categories have been fairly represented. And it can seek, as it now does not, the voicing of responsible local opinion.

When a station's license comes up for renewal, the fact might usefully be publicized well ahead of time in the local or regional press and public opinion officially invited on its record of service.

The remoteness and "inhumanity" of Washington's official world could also be reduced if hearings were held in the area — if a commissioner or other member of the FCC staff went to the community and became recognized as a human being and not as an ogre of bureaucracy. Stations obviously rendering a useful public service might be exempt, but border-line cases, designated for a hearing before renewal is sanctioned, might be judged on the spot, with the local public represented in evidence received. By such means the community could be made aware of its very real stake in its local radio station. Its sense of participation in the conduct of broadcasting would be enhanced and it would have a much better appreciation of the role of the Commission as guardian of the people's rights. Local opinion is at present only represented before the Commission by the licensee and the result is often farcical.

It has become a regrettable practice for stations appearing before the Commission to comb their listening public for affidavits, signers of petitions, letters and telegrams to support their claims. In the opinion of the Commission this is in most cases resulting only in the encumbrance of the record without any particular significance. Even a comparatively unimportant and unpopular station can, by announcements from the station and by recourse to friends, make a formidable showing which is usually more probative of the diligence of the broadcaster than of the popularity of his station.[12]

A further useful innovation might be to renew the license of stations with a doubtful record for *one year* only, returning to the community for hearings at the end of this probationary period. The station would be put on its mettle, the public would be aware of the situation, and the Commission would have a weapon at its disposal less arbitrary and fatal than the revocation, or nonrenewal of the license.[13]

Thus the fiction of tyranny and excess of zeal in the Commission dissolves before the light of facts. The just criticism of the FCC is not one of tyranny but of weakness. It is indeed difficult to see how the

[12] In the Court of Appeals, Washington, D.C., is the matter of the application of Great Lakes Broadcasting Co. *et al.*, 1928.

[13] This proposal has been adopted by the FCC, since this was written.

Commission could, anyhow, usurp its powers for long. The system of controls is too effective. No, the question raised by the facts is of an opposite nature. Why this record of timidity, inaction, and default? Because this question bears not only on the FCC's activities but on our whole system of democratic government, it is worth brief investigation.

The FCC is the guardian of our peace of mind and satisfaction at our receiving sets. It combines the role of policeman and magistrate. But no police force or police court has ever had to endure such constant and unreasonable interference with the performance of its duties. It is almost as if we had a society for the prevention of cruelty to burglars. The main pressure has come from two sides — from members of Congress and from the radio industry.

Members of Congress have scarcely ever left the Commission alone. Though few of the motions to investigate the FCC have been approved, their effect on the nerves and self-assurance of the Commission can be imagined. The FCC, too, can claim a "fear of the unknown," a sense of being "under a compulsion that is invisible."

There is good reason, also, to believe that individual members of the Congress have abused their privilege. After the passage of the 1934 Act, there was a good deal of political activity to block the appointment of the commissioners to the new agency, and *Variety* reported leading Congressmen "working tooth and nail to grab off patronage." [14] Some Congressmen have gone further. "In 1940, the Attorney General's Committee on Administrative Procedure noted that it is a widely and firmly held belief that the FCC had been subjected to constant external pressure, particularly by members of Congress. . . . As the Acheson Committee monograph points out, Congressional response to constituents in the matter of licenses and frequencies is heightened because of the political value of radio and radio broadcasters to the Congressman in his home town or state. 'Attempts by Congressmen to utilize their official positions as an excuse for special pleading . . . are made with some degree of frequency.' . . . Commenting on the report, *Variety* notes that the 'errand boy' Congressman has become increasingly active in radio matters, and that this is one of the most vicious aspects of the backdoor radio lobby in Washington." [15] Such practices advance neither the work of the Commission nor the cause and safety of our democratic system.

[14] *Congress and the Control of Radiobroadcasting*, Studies in the Control of Radio series. Harvard University Press, 1944, p. 806, by Carl J. Friedrich and Evelyn Sternberg, to whom the author is also indebted for other examples here cited.
[15] *Ibid.*, pp. 807, 808.

The net effect of this kind of logrolling has been to emasculate the FCC's will and power to act in the public interest. All the symptoms and attributes of the timid child of our allegory are deducible from this hostile environment. The FCC is in fact (and more's the pity) a textbook case of psychological frustration. The behavior of some members of the Congress is the more inexcusable when one recalls that the Act of 1934 deliberately delegated power and discretion to the Commission to interpret public interest, thus absolving it in large measure from the normal duty of a regulatory agency to refer back to Congress problems of interpretation not foreseen at the time of the drafting of the Act establishing the agency.

The radio industry has likewise applied pressure. It is commonly held to have one of the strongest and most active political lobbies in Washington. When in 1934 an amendment was moved in the Senate requiring that 25 per cent of radio time be allotted to programs on behalf of religious, educational, and other nonprofit organizations, *Variety* reported that "the NAB were in a panic checking off names of Senators and trying to pull wires and get votes." On another occasion, in 1938, even the Congressmen were appalled at the activities of the radio lobbyists. Said Representative O'Connor, "You will find difficulty in getting through the lobby because of the crowd of radio lobbyists," and Representative Connery, "Apparently the RCA is worried about a Congressional investigation. They sent a high-powered publicity agent scurrying around the halls of Congress to mold public opinion." The radio industry's trade paper has likewise assiduously built up the fiction of a tyranny in the Commission. Not all its blows have been above the belt.[16]

Such buffetings perhaps explain why the Commission has at times been short of breath. They hardly condone its long record of default. In fairness, however, we must recognize that the Commission has been both understaffed for effective supervision of radio's activities and also distracted by conflicting and exacting duties. Control over radio stations is only one of the Commission's functions. The whole sphere of communications, national and international, comes under its supervision: telegraphs, cable-wireless, and the rest. Its postwar burden will be yet greater. Television, radar, wireless telephony, facsimile broadcasting — all these will complicate, as

[16] "I have reluctantly arrived at the conclusion that there are large interests in the industry, and large but by no means all elements in the industry press which deliberately promote this fear for the purpose of creating distrust between the FCC and the working broadcasters." Commissioner Ray Wakefield in testimony at the Wheeler White hearings in December 1943.

they will make more urgent, the task of regulation
and control. The Commission has so far had no adequate research unit to make continuing and up-to-
date studies of what radio stations are doing and
what new problems of principle and policy are
emerging in a field of technical development still
in its infancy. A thorough house cleaning is overdue.
But more cleaners are needed if the job is to be well
done.

IX

FM

GIVEN THE FACTS presented in earlier chapters, only a miracle, one might say, could save us from the projection of present trends into an indefinite future. But a miracle *has* happened. Radio has a second chance. One, at least, of the restrictive influences of the past is gone — the physical. There is now opportunity for almost every listener throughout the country to enjoy that choice of programs that has so far been available only to dwellers in big cities. The moot question is whether the vested interests of radio will have the power to impose their restrictive will over the new realm of radio that science has opened up to us. Shall we muff this second chance?

"I believe that radio in a democracy must be more than an industry, more than a medium of entertainment, more than a source of revenue for those who own the facilities. . . . The testing time for broadcasting and broadcasters is just beginning."[1] That statement echoes the sentiments and lends significance (if not validity) to the arguments we have been advancing. What is the nature of the test that now confronts us?

Frequency modulation is a new technique for the transmission of sound over the air. Most people are persuaded that, except perhaps in rural areas, FM, as it is called, is destined within a few years to replace Amplitude Modulation (or AM), our present method of transmission, altogether. Within ten years, in other words, we shall all have FM receivers and none, or few, will have AM receivers.

FM transmission has three great advantages. It eliminates static and interference. (You can listen in a thunderstorm or even if you live next door to a doctor using electric apparatus.) It gives you nearly perfect fidelity of sound. (You are about to discover that you have never yet heard the "true" sound of music over the radio.) But, most priceless of all, it eliminates the traffic congestion, the shortage of frequencies, which has thus far restricted the number of stations that could operate. It is now technically possible for us to have anywhere from 3500 to 5000 additional radio stations. The implications of this fact alone are staggering.

[1] Edward R. Murrow in a broadcast on September 16, 1945.

Two conditioning factors will influence the use we make of this new chance in radio — the economic and the personal. Let us consider each in turn. Even a small FM station costs money to build and to operate. The costs, however, will be lower than for AM broadcasting. Unless other factors are allowed to intervene, many more people, with much less capital available, will have a chance to prove their mettle.[2]

If the "right" people, however you appraise them, get a fair chance to set up shop on competitive terms that do not spell ruin for them from the start, there should be opportunity to test and prove some theories of radio's scope, and listeners' responsiveness to new appeals, which the restrictive controls of our current radio setup have precluded. It is as if a new continent had been discovered, with room for all and opportunity for each. This is very heady wine and optimists had better be forewarned at once of sobering considerations.

We are not starting from scratch. AM radio has been with us for twenty years. Huge vested interests have been developed and these will not be readily

[2] An FM transmitter, according to one estimate, with 250-watt power, can be constructed for some $4500; the transmitting antennae from $300 to $3000, according to the site; studios and studio equipment and control room $4000, or considerably less. See *F.M. for Education,* issued by the U. S. Office of Education.

surrendered. For listeners the opportunities foreshadowed are giddily exciting. For the radio industry the transition from AM to FM presents a considerable financial liability (all transmitters will have to be transformed and many new ones built) and an even more serious menace.

Radio stations, up to two thirds of their total number, have through the years been absorbed by the four great networks. By affiliation of most of the best stations in most of the best localities ("best" meaning profitable), competition has been reduced to manageable proportions. By silent agreement (deriving from a common philosophy and a common purpose) each of the four networks has fished in the same pond for the same big fish — the mass radio audiences. The big fish were plentiful enough to bite at roughly the same bait (that is, the same program fare) dangled by the four anglers and have been hungry enough to drive smaller fry away to the bottom of the pond.

But what happens now? A crowd of new anglers turns up dangling a new and varied assortment of bait into the same pond. The small fry start rising in shoals and tasting the new bait. The big fish, not to be outdone by the small fry, start nibbling the new bait and those with a palate still not irretrievably impaired begin to get caught by the intruding anglers. The net effect is that more fish, by far, get caught but they get caught by far more anglers. This is not at all according to plan. The pond had been posted with the proper "Keep Off" signs but trespassers are now jostling all around it. Radio is threatened with the prospect of a fragmentation of its large mass audiences as listeners, discovering a wider variety of interests, split into smaller, though still very large, interest groups.

This is part of the problem which the Federal Communications Commission was trying to solve in 1945. How could a transition from AM to FM broadcasting be achieved with the minimum of delay and with the maximum advantage to the public? How could the increased scope for variant program service be realized with fairness at once to radio's vested interests and to newcomers in the field?

The Commission's original views as to what might be done included two important proposals. Both had the unanimous support of the whole Commission when its proposed rules and regulations on FM were first issued. Listeners, it felt, would be more readily attracted to FM (and would therefore buy FM sets more rapidly) if in the initial stages of transition it demonstrated not only its high fidelity and freedom from static but its capacity to bring listeners a richer and more varied range of programs.

The interests of the present licenses of AM frequencies were to be safeguarded by assuring each and all of them a coverage on FM as great as, if not greater than, their present coverage. None, in other words, was going to be squeezed out. But AM licenses were asked, as they developed FM broadcasting in parallel with AM, to devote two hours a day on FM to new and original programs. For the rest, they could duplicate on FM their existing programs on AM — at any rate until a majority of listeners had acquired FM sets.

At public hearings, held in June 1945, this proposal was strenuously opposed by a virtually united front of the radio industry. Their arguments were interesting and, from their point of view, not at all unreasonable. Listeners, they claimed, who bought FM receivers would still want to hear their favorite programs. When it was pointed out that listeners could do so barring two hours a day, it was contended that even this meager demonstration of new program possibilities in radio was arbitrary and superfluous as the public was entirely satisfied with what it was getting. As the president of NBC put it, "The general public are tickled to death with the American system of broadcasting. We are giving the public everything we know how to give them today. People are not going to pay to get anything different." Asked, "You

think it would be less of a waste of frequencies to
produce Charlie McCarthy on both AM and FM
than to present Charlie McCarthy on AM and then
have on FM a type of program such as a symphony
concert?" the executive vice-president of CBS said
"Yes." And a third witness added, "We feel our AM
programs are the best that long experience can devise to attract attention and hold interest."

To all these witnesses FM was "just a better means
of transmission." The idea that it might offer scope
for a more generous provision of programs, at present
few in number or nonexistent on the air, appeared
abhorrent. "We are giving the public everything we
know." To ask present radio licensees to devise two
hours of new programs a day "would compel the AM
broadcaster to divide his resources, his audience and
his revenue, without any equivalent benefit to the
listener." The small fry at the bottom of the pond,
in other words, were muddying the waters. And anyhow, as another more candid witness put it, the rule
would achieve nothing. Network affiliates would not
break their contractual obligation to carry network
programs all but uninterruptedly from 7 to 11 P.M.
If forced to comply, "the majority will do it from
6 to 7 A.M. and 11 P.M. to midnight." And what would
be the use of that?

Thus it appears we have already reached the millennium in broadcasting. Everyone is tickled to death and all we need to do is tickle the public with a higher degree of fidelity. The executive vice-president of CBS thought nothing of the argument that new programs would attract new listeners to FM. In his view the main motivating force behind the rapid purchase of FM receivers would be "the attraction of something new" (but not new programs) and the incentive of keeping up with the Joneses already attracted to the something new.

Faced by the almost universal opposition of the radio industry, the FCC went into full retreat and reversed its original, considered judgment. The rules for FM broadcasting, in the interim period of transition, are to contain no requirement for separate programing, even for two hours a day.

One member of the Commission only opposed this concession to the industry. He put it this way: —

The value of frequency modulation broadcasting does not lie solely in its superior fidelity and greater freedom from static and interference. Of equal, if not greater, importance are the new spaces which it opens up in the broadcasting spectrum and the opportunities thereby afforded of providing the public with a wider range of program choice. Because of the failure of the Commission to require any independent programing of FM stations, I am very much afraid that many FM licensees who are now operating AM stations will be inclined to regard their FM licenses primarily as insurance policies protecting their AM operations against the risks of technological development, with the result that, for several years at least, the listening public will receive little more than the same program traffic carried over improved highways. It seems to me that the use of two radio channels for only one program service is not only a waste of frequencies but will retard the development of FM broadcasting. FM will develop at the speed of the increase of listening sets in the hands of the public and, in my opinion, listeners will not be encouraged to buy FM receivers if their investment means only that they can hear a little more clearly the same programs which they now receive.

It is true that some new programs will be offered by newcomers into the broadcasting field, such as educational institutions and the comparatively few commercial newcomers having the financial means to absorb the operating losses which are to be expected until FM broadcasting becomes established, but still the AM operators should be expected to carry their full share of the burden of FM development. Their profits now are at an all-time peak, and it is not unreasonable to expect them, in the interests of the public they have undertaken to serve, to devote at least a part of these profits to the production of new programs, particularly suited to the greater fidelity of FM broadcasting.[3]

[3] Dissenting opinion of Commissioner C. J. Durr.

The second proposal originally put forward by the FCC had in mind the protection of the newcomer. It was feared that all the best transmitter sites and all the most attractive frequencies might be rapidly absorbed by present owners of AM stations unless some were held in reserve for those not able at the moment to apply for licenses. The Commission no doubt had particularly in mind the millions of men fighting for their country in the armed forces. FM, it hoped, would provide an opportunity for that increased competition on which private enterprise is held to thrive. "It is economically and socially unwise to concentrate the control of broadcasting facilities in the hands of a select few, and it is economically and socially essential to keep the door open to the fullest extent possible for newcomers." [4] It proposed, therefore, to reserve twenty "channels" from immediate assignment.

But again the radio industry was up in arms. Why, they asked, should they be called upon to make the pace, win listeners over to FM, carry the burden of the unprofitable years (while FM listeners were still too few to offer a market to advertisers) while favored newcomers could wait until the FM market proved remunerative and then move in and reap the rewards of others' labor? A great industry had been

[4] FCC Allocation Report, May 25, 1945.

built up in good faith and was now faced, if not with ruin, at any rate with a heavy burden of capital expenditure and a complex reorganization of its technical facilities. Newcomers were welcome in competition but why should they be preferentially considered? [5]

Again the Commission yielded to the industry. "The Commission does not propose to reserve any FM channels from assignment at the present time." Unto him that hath shall be given, and the dice are now heavily loaded against all newcomers.

Consider the relative position of present and future incumbents. Both are involved in the capital cost of new transmitting equipment. But the newcomer must build studios while AM radio stations must not. The newcomer must face a total or near total loss during his initial years of operation. He must produce programs, but as long as FM listeners are few he will fail to attract advertisers. AM sta-

[5] Networks advanced the same argument at the FCC hearings in 1940 on its proposed Chain Broadcasting Regulations. NBC and CBS both claimed "a kind of protected status because of their pioneering and first-comer position." "The fruits of enterprise," said CBS, "must be preserved." But on this occasion the FCC rejected the plea. "Both," it said, "have reaped and reaped richly. . . . They can hardly argue that their investment, already returned many times over, is an essential element in radio broadcasting which deserves to be protected by monopolistic rights." See Chain Broadcasting Report, p. 50.

tions are involved in no such loss. They will continue to make profits on their AM stations and by duplicating their programs on AM and FM will have no additional program costs. They have also ingeniously stacked the cards against newcomers by offering to carry their AM advertisers on their FM transmitters also — *without additional charge!* It would need a very altruistic advertiser to pay cash to a newcomer, with an FM station only, when he can reach the majority of listeners on AM and on FM too, without spending an extra penny. There was no returned veterans' representative at the hearings.

It seems clear, then, that radio is to change onto new highways but that the character of programs and the concentration of power in radio will remain substantially unchanged — except in so far as enterprise and imagination can outwit the independent local station. Here we should see some surprises. Given such developments as we propose and foreshadow in the next chapter, the little man with the large view may be the means of upsetting a good many shibboleths about what goes in radio. Thanks to the FCC, however, he will face a few years of penurious apprenticeship as price for his impudence in challenging the radio industry colossus.

New programs on independent stations may be looked for from two quarters. A number of nonprofit organizations, not out for money but for legitimate publicity, may be able to afford the cost of constructing and operating stations catering for their particular clientele. Trade-unions and labor organizations, churches, some foundations perhaps, and other similar bodies are likely to come on the air. They will not be able to compete for the mass entertainment audiences but they will reach their own loyal adherents. This is all to the good — as long as good standards of broadcasting are realized.

A second source of varied programs is the world of education. For education the FCC has wisely reserved twenty channels and the radio industry has not seen fit to challenge their decision. Twenty channels are sufficient for hundreds of educational stations all over the country. A number of state and municipal educational authorities have already applied for FM licenses. A few universities, notably Columbia University and the University of North Carolina, are likewise pioneering in this new continent of the air. Columbia is to experiment with "classes on the air in certain subjects of general appeal, such as science, sociology, anthropology, American history, international affairs, literature and language." Also with "discussions and debates on important and timely issues." The list of universities as yet aware of the potential revolution of the mind which FM broadcasting allows them to achieve is disappointingly small. One hopes that others will apply in time. The Commission will not be able to reserve channels indefinitely. If educators default, their heritage will revert to the commercial broadcasters.

No one can foretell how real the promise of educational broadcasting is likely to prove. As we shall see in the next chapter, we have a melancholy story to look back on regarding the fate of educational stations in AM days. The lessons of the past need to be taken to heart. Educational broadcasting will not prosper, even in the classroom (and it would be a thousand pities if it were limited to school broadcasting), without adequate financing, expert and well-paid staff — writers, producers, engineers — and a pooling of resources. The plethora of stations that can now be constructed may well involve a dissipation of efforts and a dilution of the quality of programs unless educators realize the limitations, as well as the wealth, of their local resources and cooperate for the mutual benefit of all. Nor will the dry bones of educational subject matter live unless the breath of talented writing and imaginative treatment is blown into them. There are not many masters of the art of radio-writing and production. The danger for radio education is the overconfidence of amateurs and provincial pride and exclusiveness.

David can kill Goliath with a slingshot but his aim must be sure. He must know how to reach the vital spot.

The inherent weaknesses of our current system of broadcasting are, it seems, to be perpetuated. The radio industry, more fearful of the influx of new competition than mindful of a new, golden opportunity to enrich and diversify its program services, wants to restrict the miracle of FM to the improvement of radio's highways. It has prevailed on the FCC to put the newcomer at a crippling competitive disadvantage and to deprive the public of an expansion of program service.

For several years to come we shall have AM and FM stations, but we shall have little new by way of programs. We shall have hundreds of new highways but the program traffic will be virtually the same as now. In commercial broadcasting a miracle of opportunity has been converted into a new patent right for radio's present vested interests. The situation, except for the unproved possibilities of nonprofit broadcasting, remains essentially the same.

We face, as before, entrenched interests preoccupied with profit, a Commission, as before, fearful of exercising its regulatory responsibilities in the public's interest, and a public largely ignorant of what is going on and unorganized for action.

X

A Plan for the Future

IT IS ALWAYS easier to see what is wrong than to know what is right. A wrong we recognize; we aspire to the good. History is largely a record of protest and rejection. The reformer, once his wrong is righted, acquires a disconcerted look. We, in our turn, come now to planning. Even without confidence of its acceptance, the plan is worth projecting as illustrating the many-sided role of the public in keeping radio straight.

We, the listeners, are at present the sleeping partners in the great enterprise of radio. It is time we woke up. Neither the industry, nor the FCC, nor the Congress, will function effectively without knowledge of the listeners' positive demands and a feeling of their active support and critical awareness. The industry, as we have seen, has employed a fiction to equate public interest with concern for profits. The Commission has been timid in testing public interest by formulating principles that express our unspecified desires. The thinking of Congress has been too frequently off the top of its head, neither grounded in nor informed sufficiently of public needs. One reason for all this is that exports of our considered judgment have been deficient. But imports, of the raw material of knowledge, are the prerequisites of any export of processed judgment. What is wrong with our present import trade?

If we are to know more about what goes on in radio, we must hear more about it. What's good and bad in radio's program service is, or should be, primarily the public's concern. But questions of good taste and of artistic merit require public canvassing if they are to graduate from the level of purely subjective opinion to that of collective judgment.

For such a canvassing, we need a corps of informed and responsible critics. While plays performed in the "legitimate" theater (having comparatively small audiences) and books, even on abstruse subjects, are regularly reviewed in the press, similar reviews of radio's best productions, performed before an unseen audience of millions, receive only occasional and limited notice. Current press publicity for radio programs is useful, but limited, both in its extent and in the function it performs.[1] Responsible press criti-

---

[1] A survey shows that only 25 per cent of daily papers publish radio program listings without charge and that 93 per cent of these have some financial interest in radio.

cism of radio programs can do much more; it can raise the standards of public appreciation and stimulate the free and unfettered development of what some, at any rate, believe to be a new art form of singular promise.

Apart from program reviews, there are the broader questions of policy, on some of which this book has touched. The philosophy of the radio industry, the policy of the Commission, the new problems raised by scientific discovery — all these are our concern. However, beyond occasional articles in monthly magazines like the *Atlantic Monthly* and *Harper's Magazine*, some useful but limited comment in weeklies (the *New York Times* Sunday edition, for example), we get little to inform or stimulate us. The best, the most courageous, and the most comprehensive criticism now published appears in *Variety*, a weekly trade journal unfortunately limited in its circulation outside the show business. Every listener would profit from reading it.

Our provincial press is for the most part silent on a subject that probably touches more people's interests than most. Very few papers indeed even give us more than the bare titles of programs on the air. Press and radio are still playing as rivals. There is not only room for both, but the two are complementary. More people would turn to their papers if they could learn more from them about what dates to keep with their radios each day. Many people hear something over the air and turn to their newspapers to confirm or supplement it.

The interest in radio is wide enough to justify a journal (a monthly or perhaps even a weekly) devoted exclusively to the subject. If successfully launched, it would stimulate competition. Interest, once revealed, would get attention. The time seems ripe for such a pioneering venture.

Such a journal could help satisfy numerous interests. It would provide an outlet for listeners' opinions. Its correspondence column should be full and lively. The paper could become influential as a channel for voicing public opinion.

Radio programs could be criticized. Standards of taste could be raised. There are many who read, for instance, reviews of books which they never buy or borrow. The critic interprets more than his immediate subject. He interprets life, manners, values, attitudes, and gives articulate expression to our own unformulated thoughts and feelings. The best critics are read, in part at least, for what they, as perceptive and sensitive persons, have to say. Their subject is often as much a convenient and timely context as the central point of interest.

The journal's praise of a broadcast might encourage that repetition of better programs that is so overdue. Local affiliated stations might be more wary of substitution for programs that are known to be widely popular. Thus public opinion might come into its own.

Through such a journal, the force of example might gradually encourage the adoption or imitation of sound and useful practices. We could hear of programs in other countries in which new techniques or new subjects have been successfully handled. In our own country, there are many programs, locally originated, which, once others heard about them, could be adopted or adapted. Successful local programs could get national publicity. We might well get more instances of the nationwide broadcasting of such a program as that prepared (as a commencement exercise) by a high school in Minnesota, first broadcast locally, then over the Blue Network. Other communities might emulate such enterprise as that of Syracuse, New York, where not only are listeners organized, but the University co-operates with the local radio station in presenting local problems on the air. "Syracuse on Trial" is a broadcast series which every community throughout America could copy with advantage to healthy democratic life. Radio here works with and for the community, and in so doing works for democracy.

The general interest in radio personalities offers endless scope for popular articles. So do articles on the technical side of radio. FM and television provide a fresh fillip to the amateur radio fan's enthusiasm of earlier days. Adults and high school children alike provide a market for such articles. We are born mechanics.

There is great need, also, for more specialized service. The coming of FM raises, particularly for educators, complicated problems of construction and maintenance. Few know how to apply correctly for a license. The question of costs, the techniques of operation — these and like questions could be answered. There is also the more specialized field of what might be called the higher criticism of radio — broad reviews of policy, criticisms of FCC decisions, comment on trade practices and trends. These need popular interpretation. Acceptance of principles is the sheet anchor of unity and of consent. The journal could provide a continuing channel for the interpretation of democratic principles in a familiar and vital context. Whether we get such a journal or not, we need, in any case, much wider attention to radio in current journals. New York's newspaper *P.M.* has pioneered but few have followed the trail.

Not all the facts about radio are easily accessible. Some have to be dug up, more have to be correlated, analyzed, interpreted. Radio research is still in its infancy. Apart from fine work done by the Columbia Broadcasting System (Frank Stanton's collaboration with Paul Lazarsfeld in the "Radio Research" series is an example), the industry offers little to the public. There is, perhaps, no reason why it should. Much research is anyhow better undertaken independently, unhampered by the risk of revealing trade secrets or exposing unwelcome facts. This is pre-eminently a field in which radio's "third estate," the public, should be active.

Such research is particularly desirable at universities. Leaders in the field are Columbia University (where the office of Radio Research, directed by Paul Lazarsfeld, has done a great pioneering job), and Ohio State University. At Harvard, Professor Carl Friedrich has produced several useful studies and Professor Sandage a book on radio retail advertising.

But only the surface of the ground has yet been scratched. Radio is a huge commercial enterprise, a political and social force already affecting us profoundly. Our tastes and attitudes, our emotional state, our intellectual outlook and our relations with foreign countries, all come under radio's magnetic influence. It already has a full and lurid history. Its history keeps growing. It has occupied the time of our legislators in Congress, taxed the discriminating faculties of lawyers. It is a part of our law, our history, and our culture.

If we are to have more critics, a radio journal, and, in due course, an informed public, sustenance is needed. The reporter and the critic want evidence. The social philosopher and the psychologist (amateurs like ourselves included) need cases and context. There is room, then, for a vast expansion of studies in radio. The market for them is wide open.

To reach this great, potential market, the research must be conveniently and attractively packaged. We have too much dry-as-dust scholarship, too much sheer piling up of facts regardless of their meaning and implications. We have statistics galore, a profession of enumerators trying (vainly, one still hopes) to persuade us that figures and facts are synonymous. (Arithmetic is not enough. The human equation cannot be stated in Arabic numerals.) Research and interpretation in such a social context as that of radio are inseparable.

Radio, indeed, offers a promising field for a new kind of research writing — accurate but not abstruse, elaborate but only if relevantly so. We need analysis combined with critical acumen, study related to and inspired by a social philosophy (the democratic philosophy will do) and a sense of purpose. And we can do with writing that observes the timely precept, "Think like a wise man, but communicate in the language of the people." Universities by undertaking such research can reach to the people, or at least to the people's intermediaries for whom we're pleading. The dry bones of scholarship can live again.

Probably we need a Central Radio Research Institute, drawing on and influencing studies undertaken all over the country, saving duplicate effort and co-ordinating these dispersed activities. There would be practical advantage in having such a focal point to refer to and draw on and to which to suggest needed research projects. Anybody writing about radio at the present time knows the difficulty of finding out where to turn for wanted information. We need a warehouse for our imported raw material.

With the war's end, education is likely to be subject to a dangerous and shortsighted form of pressure for concentration on vocational training. The need for more vocational training goes without question. The danger is in the implied threat to study of the so-called humanities. Education's first duty is to teach us how to live, not how to earn a living. We need both kinds, but the first foremost.

Just as we need a new kind of research writing, so we probably need a new kind of education. Short of the college level, so far from there being any need, there is possibly positive danger in keeping humanistic and practical subjects in separate and watertight compartments. Learning how to live and how to earn a living can perhaps best be taught simultaneously with emphasis on their inextricable nature. Business training, for instance, is less likely to result in the dollar philosophy of Mr. Ryan and his associates (and can be more, rather than less, efficient) if students are given some inkling of what business efficiency means in a wider social context than that of profits and reduced man hours per unit of production. More men and women in industry "with a personal preference for poetry or opera" are likely to mean better, certainly more responsible, business.

One of the expanding fields for employment (and therefore, presumably, for vocational training) is radio. Many schools and colleges already offer radio courses, some few have radio workshops in which the elements of radio production, script writing, and the rest are taught.[2] Their expansion is not our main thought, but rather an expansion (in and out of radio

[2] Before the war, 400 colleges offered special courses in radio. Significantly, only 24 offered courses in radio education and *only two dealt with the social implications of radio.* Thus, even before the war, the bias toward vocational training (one third of the courses were technical, one third were speech and drama courses) was already marked. See *Service Bulletin of the Federal Radio Education Committee,* October 1940.

workshops) of the training in some of the fundamental disciplines of education to include the use of radio as an illustrative context for these disciplines. To purists, such a notion will be anathema. The writer knows from practical experience how immediate is the interest — and surprise — provoked by using radio as an illustration of philosophical, sociological, logical, and aesthetic points. What seemed remote becomes immediate and near, what was thought theoretical or purely intellectual acquired all the excitement and relevance of the practical when treated in this way. Consider some examples.

Radio advertising plugs provide ideal illustrations for logic, for spotting the difference between straight and crooked thinking and verbal expression. The writer has similarly watched the effect on a psychology class of the playing of a record of the "Men from Mars" and the subsequent use of Hadley Cantril's study of the emotional reactions to that famous and innocent indiscretion of the radio. For sociologists, soap operas provide revealing case histories of maladjustment and escapist daydreaming among millions of women. The political question of the proper relation between government and industry is similarly illustrated in an urgent, contemporary field by radio. Writing for radio is altogether relevant to the teaching of English literature. In radio workshops, this may incidentally lead to the recruitment to the industry of new talent and new ideas for the perfection of a new art form.

In ordinary nonvocational classes, concerned with such disciplines as the above, the use of radio as illustration will not only enliven interest in the subject, it may indirectly achieve something far more important. It may raise a new generation of listeners with higher standards of expectation of what the radio offers, a stronger sales resistance to unwarranted or deceptive advertising claims, and a much broader, more alert conception of radio's role and immense possibilities. Schools and colleges may be decisive in the contribution they thus indirectly make to the future quality and integrity of radio. Radio as a tool of education is an essential part of the plan for the future. The combined effect of the activities we have proposed should be to give us adequate imports of much needed information.

We have referred to the listener as the sleeping partner in radio. It is time for us not only to wake up but to awake to the modern world, avail ourselves of the techniques which today secure for social groups a voice in the conduct of affairs. It is not enough to be informed, alert, and conscious of what we're after. To get what we want we have to organize. Organization is the modern means of imposing our collective will. Our country is too big for the voice of any one of us to carry across it. Our individual voice in any case has small significance unless it echoes those of others.

The radio industry, as we have seen, is strongly organized. It has huge resources for publicizing its point of view, an overpowerful lobby in Washington, and a common, if imperfect, philosophy. All this spells strength. Radio is a powerful pressure group. It is very much awake. The listener sleeps on.

There is nothing wrong with pressure groups — except their misuse and a monopoly on pressure. Until fairly recent times, pressure groups were virtually synonymous with the possession of wealth. The moneyed interests had things their own way, and both monopolized the area of barometric pressure and abused it. The result was stormy weather. One of the encouraging signs of health and vitality in our democracy today is the growth of pressure groups bespeaking other than moneyed interests. Labor is organized. The NCPAC is developing sustained political awareness. The League of Women Voters, teachers' associations, and similar pressure groups are trying to piece the complicated jigsaw puzzle of organized society together into a harmonious pattern for the benefit of all. The listener must do the same for radio. "Get what you like or you will grow to like what you get." Fascism is the ultimate upshot of growing to like what you get. That is why all this is so important.

How can the listener get organized? The strength of an organization is proportionate to the bond of interests among its members. Industry is strongly organized not only because it has wealth but because of its common interest in acquiring wealth. Labor grows in strength as workers pool the common interest between them to improve their lot. Organization springs from the desire to do something.

The trouble with radio is that, at present, the sense of a common interest is weak. Listening is, or seems, a passive role. We think of radio more as a luxury than as a social necessity. Jack Benny and Charlie McCarthy do not seem to furnish an adequate occasion for all of us to get together to do something. As long as we think of radio in such terms rather than as a force of almost terrifying import (the virtual equivalent of the atomic bomb in the realm of ideas), the prospect of effective organization is poor. That is why we have insisted on the priority of imports, of getting enough people aware of what is going on and what is in the wind to stimulate a desire to do something about it.

Some listeners have already imported enough

knowledge about radio to make them anxious to do something about it. In various sections of the country, radio listeners' councils have been formed to influence the policy of their local radio stations. What we need is a spreading of this movement until every community in which a radio station exists has its pressure group organized.

The listeners' council has an important and quite practicable role to play. Its first function is to keep the flow of imports going, to spread awareness among the people of the profound influence being exerted, day in and day out, by radio on public tastes and attitudes.

Its second task is to organize the export of the listeners' considered judgment on the facts presented to them. It provides the much needed channel through which to convey to the radio industry the wishes of its vast but inarticulate clientele. A specific task is the promotion of sustaining programs and the representation of the nonprofit organizations whose activities are at present so poorly and infrequently presented on the air.

A good listeners' council, indeed, will make a point of electing to its membership the representatives of existing pressure groups whose bonds are already strong through the common interest of a common activity. Radio's main defect. as an occasion for organization — the listeners' passive role — can thus be turned to advantage. It can be shown to be anything but passive, an unrivaled opportunity for advancing the interests of the associated pressure groups.

Their association in a listeners' council, moreover, will have this further advantage. Different, and more particularly rival, pressure groups will get acquainted on the council. A reconciliation of viewpoints may result. Co-operation may take the place of competition. In any case, rival pressure groups (labor and industry, for instance) will find common interests outside their area of conflict and will become associated in common enterprises — in planning programs, say, for better health, better housing, better education. A gradual leavening of the lump of social solidarity will develop through the catalytic agency of radio.

The ultimate expansion of listener councils, to embrace all or most communities in which a radio station exists, will see radio's third estate come into its own at last. Then, perhaps, will be the time for a federation resulting in the effective representation of the listener in the nation's Capital. We have suggested in an earlier chapter that Washington, in the guise of the FCC, move out to meet the people. We, the people, can repay the call and meet Washington halfway through the formation of a national listeners' advisory council, meeting, say quarterly, with the Commission to acquaint it of national, regional, and local needs as voiced in the different local radio councils. When hearings on station license renewals are called for, the local listeners' councils should give evidence. When new problems of regulatory policy arise (such as FM or television or a new bill in Congress) the national advisory council could prepare its brief, present the listeners' point of view.

Such associations are inevitably cumbersome in their operation. Too often they are ineffective. The appointment of committees has frequently proved a convenient device for silencing current discontent, and doing nothing more about it. But the risk has to be taken.

We need a production center for public service programs. The case for its establishment rests on some aspects of the past history of public service broadcasting which we might briefly review.

The story of educational radio stations is, at worst, one of sheer professional incompetence. At best, it is the record of a courageous struggle against almost hopeless odds. The muddled thinking about radio of many educators, the unhappy influence of politics (as it affected state university radio stations in particular), the opposition of commercial broadcasters

— these and other influences have contributed to a sorry story.[3] Twenty years ago there were 176 educational stations. Today only 30 are left.

At the risk of oversimplifying a complex problem, one might say that the basic trouble with educational stations has been a vicious circle of cause and effect from which few have as yet entirely escaped. Inadequate funds have resulted in the appointment of men as radio directors with insufficient grasp either of what education is all about or of effective radio techniques. The consequence has been that, at university stations at any rate, with rare exceptions, most members of the faculty have remained unconvinced that radio is anything but a means of diluting the elixir of pure scholarship. The relatively few who saw its possibilities were reluctant to submit themselves to a new and exacting discipline — that of writing and speaking for the radio. They neither trusted their radio mentors (often with very good reason) nor believed that speaking at a microphone is different from and harder than lecturing to a class. The result was poor programs and negligible audiences. There are, of course, exceptions. Stations like WHA at the University of Wisconsin and WOI at Ames,

[3] The story is admirably told in *Radiobroadcasting and Higher Education*, C. J. Friedrich, Harvard Studies in Control of Radio, No. 4, May 1942.

Iowa, have beaten commercial radio at its own game and made a deserved name for themselves. But the exceptions only prove the rule.

We have already seen the problem, inherent in the necessity of being on the air for sixteen hours a day, of maintaining a continuing high standard of programs. The material is limitless, but its unearthing and conversion into program form require a very high degree of skill and imagination. It is no accident that stomach ulcers are almost an occupational disease in radio. The pace is fast and relentless.

With a generous band of FM frequencies reserved for educational stations, public service broadcasting gets its second chance. Will history repeat itself? Twenty years hence, shall we witness yet again the taking over of these frequencies by the commercial stations with their supposed know-how? Public interest, and all the machinery of planning we have proposed to foster it, will not suffice to avert this calamity if public service programs fail in quality and attractive power. We shall be wise to take time by the forelock and profit now by past experience.

There is already evidence that educators intend to take FM more seriously than they did AM broadcasting. Public service broadcasting will almost certainly be more generously financed and better operated. But there remains another danger — that of dispersed effort, the chronic defect of men of good will. The contention that the public will respond, in time, to "serious" subjects has still to be proved, at any rate on a scale large enough to silence skeptics. It would be madness not to give what we must still call an experiment the best chance for success by ensuring the highest possible standards of program writing and production. There is not enough talent to go around. It must be pooled. The means of such a pooling are available.

For the day which the great networks, anxious to maintain their virtual monopoly over the conduits for radio talent, have for so long sought to defer is here. One of radio's greatest needs can now be met. Through transcriptions, an independent outlet for creative writers is available, unfettered by the advertisers' fear of giving anyone offense or their narrow preconceptions of "what goes." Quality programs of enduring interest (for repeated use), or tailormade for special occasions or particular localities, can be made available to all.

But who is going to write them, produce and act them? Educators and others interested in radio's public service need to establish rapidly (others will soon be in the field) a radio production center, to undertake the specific task of building up the market for public service programs by quality production. This may yet prove to be a revolution in broadcasting, and, consequently, in the advancement of our culture and the perfection of democracy. Some of the practical aspects of the center's establishment are worth sketching in. The primary market for the center's output would be public service FM and AM stations. A secondary (and ultimately lucrative) market will be local commercial stations as the merit of the center's products is progressively demonstrated. There will be some scope for exports to countries abroad.

The staff of the center need not be large. Even half a dozen writers of real talent could work miracles, supported by an equivalent team of producers concerned to heave radio out of its artistic rut. They will need adequate remuneration, more than a pittance. But the salaries offered to a few top-notch writers and producers in commercial radio are not necessary. Artists are not gold diggers. Many writers and producers in commercial radio today would gladly sacrifice a fortune for artistic freedom. There will be those who, returning from the war, will feel nauseated by the commercialism that has been superimposed on the integrity of self-expression. They will go to great lengths to avoid a return to the old humiliating bondage. Many will have new thoughts, fresh vision to communicate, tempered and refined in the fire of war's experience. Public service broadcasting and the production center will attract them.

Production costs will not be high. Stars and their astronomical salaries are not necessary to good casting. This is a fetish and a fiction imposed on us by commercial radio. There are already numerous instances of programs by unknown writers and producers presented with unknown casts which have won larger audiences than competing programs in the big-money category.

The scope of programs is as wide as a writer's imagination and awareness of social issues. Years of work could be devoted to making good the deficiencies of commercial radio alone. Programs for children, designed to interest them in other subjects than those of murder, crime, and detection; the still unanswered craving for helpful information on health; democracy in action and on trial; service to nonprofit organizations; history, science, and art; the new problems of the global family of nations — the list is endless.

It is most desirable that the center be quickly self-supporting. An initial grant-in-aid from one of the Foundations might be sought. Salaries and production costs not being high, a quick return is likely on the sale of transcriptions. A modest annual subscription from member stations in the public service field would provide a steady revenue. With the center organized on a nonprofit basis, the budget could probably be easily balanced. A favorable balance would go to the increase of staff and production. Training courses for students, in writing and production for radio, could be organized and would provide an added source of revenue. The growth of FM public service stations will necessitate such training. The danger of which we must continuously warn ourselves is that of dispersed, diluted effort. A pooling of the best talent available is the soundest insurance of the program quality that will be needed.

Such are components of the plan for the future, first tracings of a blueprint that others can improve and elaborate. Our purpose has been to show that radio's third estate can and must come into its own. But to do so it must organize.

INDEX

Index